The TREASURES of CHRISTMAS

The TREASURES of CHRISTMAS

The Guideposts Family Christmas Book

Abingdon Press   Nashville

The Treasures of Christmas—
The Guideposts Family Christmas Book

Copyright © 1982 by Guideposts Associates, Inc.
Abingdon edition published 1983

All rights reserved. No part of this publication may be reproduced, stored in a retrieval system, or transmitted, in any form or by any means, electronic, mechanical, photocopying, recording, or otherwise, without the written permission of Guideposts Associates, Inc., Carmel, New York 10512.

Every attempt has been made to credit the sources of copyrighted material used in this book. If any such acknowledgment has been inadvertently omitted or miscredited, receipt of such information would be appreciated.

Printed in the United States of America.

Book and cover design: Elizabeth Woll
Cover photograph: J. Gerald Smith

CREDITS: "A Lasting Christmas" from *Something Beautiful* by Garnett Ann Schultz. Reprinted in January, 1972 Guideposts Magazine. Used by permission./"Make a Little Manger" by Barbara Gooden. Reprinted from Guideposts Magazine. Copyright © 1976 by Guideposts Associates, Inc./ "How to Make a Jesus Tree." Reprinted from Guideposts Magazine. Copyright © 1976 by Guideposts Associates, Inc./ "The Land Between the Rivers" from *Through Many Windows* by Arthur Gordon. Copyright © 1983 by Arthur Gordon. Published by Fleming H. Revell Co., Old Tappan, New Jersey. Used by permission.

Table of Contents

Treasures from the Heart   7

Treasures from the Spirit   19

Treasures from the Hearth   55

INTRODUCTION

THIS season we bring you treasures —Christmas treasures. And this Family Christmas Book comes to say, "We treasure *you!*" most of all. And we want to share from out of our Christmas bounty with you and yours.

- *Treasures from the Heart* is a Christmas Gift Exchange filled with gift ideas from hands as well as hearts. Special prayers and poems will lighten your spirit as you celebrate His birth this Holy Season.
- *Treasures from the Spirit* is a Fireside Reader full of new Christmas stories to delight your family and loved ones — and not just on Christmas Day!
- *Treasures from the Hearth* is a Festive Food Sampler filled with our Guideposts writers' favorite holiday recipes to help make your Christmas table fun and exciting, and tasty, too!

As you receive the greatest Treasure — the birth of God's only Son — may *The Treasures of Christmas* warm your heart and inspire you to make this your most blessed Christmas ever.

May His love and peace reign in your midst this Holy Season and all through the coming year.

The Editors

Treasures from the Heart

A Christmas Gift Exchange

A Christmas List

"Ask," He said, "and you shall receive."
When you're nine years old, your heart can believe.
"Give me a doll that drinks and sleeps."
I asked, but oh, I didn't receive.

"Ask," He said, "and you shall receive."
I was young and in love, it was Christmas Eve.
"Give me the heart of that special boy."
I asked, but oh, I didn't receive.

"Ask," He said, "and you shall receive."
Money was scarce but I tried to believe.
"Give us enough for the gifts on our list."
I asked, but oh, I didn't receive.

"Ask," He said, "and you shall receive."
Sorting my values, I began to perceive.
"Give me Your Son. Let Him shine through me."
I asked, and lo, I began to receive…

More than I'd ever dared to believe
Treasures unmeasured, blessings undreamed,
All I'd asked or hoped to achieve.
"Ask," He said, "and you shall receive."

Marilyn Morgan Helleberg

Christmas-Like Hearts

The world at Christmas,
    is fresh and new;
I wish it could linger
    all year through.

Then the shine of Christmas
    in a wondrous way,
Could send its brightness
    each passing day;

And after this season
    as the New Year starts,
We would keep on giving
    with Christmas-like hearts.

June Masters Bacher

Grandmother's Christmas Angel

LIKE most kids, I heard lots of warnings, in December, about being good because Santa was coming, but Grandmother didn't talk about Santa much. Instead, she used to tell us about a beautiful angel named Amiah, who went around every year, just before Christmas, looking for the perfect birthplace for the Baby Jesus.

Amiah wasn't looking for a palace or a church or even a manger. She was looking for a warm and loving human heart. Grandmother said *that* was the perfect birthplace for God's Son. Then she'd ask if we knew of any hearts that might be available. I can remember trying especially hard to be loving, as Christmas drew near, in the hope that *my* heart might be picked. I guess I didn't realize then, that Jesus could be born in millions of hearts at the same time.

Still, about this time every year, I think about Amiah, and I seem to hear Grandmother's voice saying "Is your heart warm and loving enough to be chosen as the birthplace of Jesus *this* year?

Marilyn Morgan Helleberg

Surprise Packages

OR my mother, creating Christmas for three children during the depression years meant working within a strict budget. The gaily-wrapped gifts that awaited us beneath the Christmas tree were generally of a practical nature: flannel shirts and warm wool scarves, slippers and mittens needed to curb the chill of an Ohio winter. But we never felt the least deprived, for there were other presents, too. Big or little, bright or plain in their brown paper, these were the boxes that held our childhood dreams. They were empty.

With a dab of paste, a dash of paint, a handful of scraps, a heartful of determination, Mom transformed cardboard cartons into castles and doll houses, oatmeal boxes into doll cradles, apple crates into cupboards or cars. We were always delighted to find these "surprise packages" on Christmas morning, better by far than anything bought from a store.

Now, close to half a century later, I, too, am recycling old boxes, remembering holidays past, and restoring some of my mother's Christmas spirit. For I've begun to understand what those "empty" boxes really held. They were filled to the top with love.

I begin my own Big Box Hunt just after Thanksgiving. This is the time that cardboard cartons really come into season, for merchants are busy unpacking holiday supplies and discarding boxes of all shapes and sizes. They're as happy to have the bulky containers off their hands as I am to lay hands on them.

Last Christmas, a stove carton became a candy house, straight out of "Hansel and Gretel." We pulled the end flaps of the box up and taped it to form a pitched roof. We painted it pink and adorned it with real, good-to-eat gingerbread boys and candy canes, affixed with powdered sugar frosting. We cut a door in one side, much too small for any grown-up, but just the right size to admit a four-year-old and friend.

Another year, we fashioned a similar carton into a puppet theatre. We covered the box with contact paper, attached a sequin-studded marquee to the top, and cut a proper stage opening into the side. Curtains sewed to brass rings hung from a wooden dowel, to slip open dramatically when the show began or draw hastily if the star got the giggles.

"Good things come from small packages" is worth remembering, too. If there are little children on your Christmas list, look for little boxes. Smaller cartons are readily available at most stores, and the more collected the merrier. A dozen or so, taped shut and covered with stick-on paper make light, safe oversize building blocks. Perhaps others might wish to share one of my own childhood favorites: a pull-toy train. Mine was simply shoe boxes strung together, but each "gondola car" was boldly numbered from one to ten. As I transported favorite stuffed animals across the floor, I learned to count in the bargain.

For me, a special sort of magic goes into the making and the giving of Surprise Packages. Last Christmas, my seven-year-old grandchild said to me "Your presents aren't really surprises at all, Nana, because I always know what's going to be inside the box. ME!"

Perhaps, in a few decades, she'll discover that a lot of me was also tucked inside those empty boxes.

Shirley Climo

A Pre-Christmas Prayer

ORD, I went shopping today in my favorite store, the one that stocks that lovely china and vases and *bric-a-brac*. I was Christmas shopping for gifts for three friends. But I came home empty-handed. Something in the store stopped me. Or, I should say — something that was *not* in the store stopped me.

All year, Lord, the statuette has been there on the shelf that holds the blown glass figures of birds and small animals and flowers. So many times I've admired it, the Good Shepherd carrying His lamb. Today it was gone, and I asked the clerk about it.

"We had to put it out of the way," she said. "We

needed the space to display more Christmas merchandise."

I stood there, thinking about that, Lord. Put Jesus out of the way to make room for things that would be used to celebrate His birthday? That just didn't seem right.

Then I thought about my home — the big gaily decorated tree in the living room, the candles on the mantel, the wreath on the door, the poinsettia on the hall table. *The crèche packed in a box in the attic.* There hadn't seemed any place to put it!

I'm going up now to unpack it, Lord. And I will set it up in the most prominent room in the house. After all, what good are the candles or the tree or anything else — even life itself — without our Blessed Saviour's presence?

Drue Duke

Make A Little Manger

There was no room in the inn
    For me,
Will you make a little manger
    In your heart?
Into this warm and lighted haven
    Will you bring Someone cold,
And lonely, and friendless?
    Thus love will be born again
Beneath the star!

Barbara Gooden

Christmas Finger Prints

YOU can — you *do* — own your own private "printing" press!

This year why don't you and your family — all ages — design your own original greeting cards for the holidays? They will be different from anybody else's because no two sets of finger prints are exactly the same. And that is what you will be using.

First, choose any kind of white or colored paper you wish to use. You will also need a felt-tip-pen and an ink pad. And, of course, your non-identical printing press.

Just place your thumb or finger on the ink pad — hard. Then press the inked finger on the paper, rolling just a little from left to right. Continue adding prints until you have created a design — a Christmas Tree, a cross, an animal, a star, a shepherd — there's no end to the holiday pictures you can create with your finger prints.

Use the felt-tipped pen to outline your design and add such touches as a crook for the shepherd, lights on the Christmas tree, streams of light from the star. Let your imagination run wild and your friends will know immediately they are receiving something very special this Christmas. And for you and your family it can be a warm memory of another Christmas shared.

June Masters Bacher

To A Friend at Christmas

He knew we needed someone
to share each happy day.
To be a source of courage
when troubles come our way.
Someone who is true to us
together or apart,
Someone whose love we'll always hold
and treasure in our hearts.

Anthony Guagenti

How to Make a Jesus Tree

MARGARET SIMPSON of Eufaula, Oklahoma, doesn't know where she got the idea. All she knows is that when the time came to decorate the family's customary five-foot tree last Christmas, the same thought kept running through her mind, "It's Jesus's birthday. It's Jesus's birthday."

And suddenly she simply didn't want to use the same old Christmas decorations again. She wanted new ones, white ones, ones that reminded her of the Bible and of Jesus. Margaret's four-year-old granddaughter, Regan Leigh, liked the idea, too, and quite by chance suggested one of the first new decorations — a tiny loaf of bread from her dollhouse.

"Jesus is the bread of life!" Margaret exclaimed, and that led her to think of Regan Leigh's little toy lamps as the "lamp unto my feet," and a fleecy sheep as the "Lamb of God," and silver stars as "the bright and morning star." Soon the two of them were decorating the tree and talking about the Bible simultaneously.

Margaret went into shops in Eufaula and McAlester and Muskogee, asking for Christian-symbol decorations, but the shopkeepers would shake their heads; no one had asked for such a thing before. So she would go home and adapt some more, until by Christmas Eve her tree was shimmering with white lights (for purity), while white angels danced and butterflies (for the Resurrection) rested gently on the green branches. It was a wondrous sight, this thing she called her Jesus Tree, one that Margaret Simpson will re-create for her family this year, and in the years to come.

And who knows, someday Regan Leigh might be decorating a similar tree for her own grandchildren saying "Now these white doves are for the Holy Spirit, and these shiny staffs for the Good Shepherd, and these...."

After-Christmas Presents

IT is June. Outside the flowers are blooming, the sun is shining, and I am enjoying a Christmas present.

Last summer, Danny, the little boy from down the street, asked if he could mow my lawn for two dollars.

Poor little guy, I thought, *probably trying to earn a little money.* He would have no way of knowing how small a retired teacher's check could be in these days of inflation.

My yard is small. I could mow it myself. And two dollars was more than I could really afford. I had to turn him down.

Then came fall and the winter snow, and the lawn was forgotten.

Christmas Eve I was hanging a wreath on my door when Danny came again.

"Well now, " I said, smiling at him, "I do not believe the lawn needs mowing today."

"I brought you a Christmas present," he said, handing me an envelope. Then looking a little embarrassed he quickly said goodbye.

I opened the letter and I shall never forget the contents, written in a childish hand.

Dear neighbor:
I have a present for you. Next summer I will mow your lawn all summer. Merry Christmas.
Danny

Danny has done far more than mow my lawn this summer. He has taught me that the gift worth giving is the gift of self. This Christmas I will have gifts for *my* neighbors, little favors that I can do for them throughout the year.

I hope, like me, they will all be enjoying my Christmas gifts when flowers are blooming and the sun is shining.

Laura Norman

God's Christmas Autograph

On Christmas Eve I saw
    God's autograph in the snow —
Tiny creature tracks so fine,
    All lacy in a row.

And with the dazzling Christmas dawn,
    My eyes did then behold.
God's signature grown ever dear,
    Etched in sunlight gold.

Rosalyn Hart Finch

The Glory of Christmas

Give thanks to the baby asleep in the hay,
For it's Jesus who gave us our first Christmas Day.
A king in disguise, God sent Him to men,
Revealed to our hearts, He comes again.

Lord of the galaxies as well as our earth,
A hymn of the Universe celebrates His birth.
He gives us His Spirit, His kingdom's within,
His peace can be ours by believing in Him.

His truth is a flame that ignites young souls,
He is comfort to men for whom the bell tolls,
He restores an image both marred and grown dim,
He's a constant wonder to those who love Him.

As we wrap up our presents to give them away,
We do this because of that First Christmas Day,
When the Lord of all glory and beauty and wealth,
Came to earth as a Baby to give us Himself.

Laverne Riley O'Brien

A Christmas Tree — for the Birds, Too!

THE little birds of the Holy Land were once remembered at Christmas by sheaves of grain placed on housetops, so that the sparrows could share the joyous season.

Later, according to legend, children in Stockholm gathered packages from the festive tree beside the great stone fireplace inside, while the birds collected their sweetmeats from the evergreen outside. So began the practice of the birds' Christmas tree, a charming custom you and your family may enjoy reviving.

If you have any tree in your yard, it would look inviting looped with colorful come-and-eat-me garlands for hungry little birds. Or what about the artificial tree in the attic you have planned to discard? Give it to the birds! Be sure to "plant" it right in front of a much-used window, and your act of goodness is sure to bring a flock of rewards.

To prepare a delectable treat for the birds, purchase suet at the market. Prepare a basic syrup of one cup of sugar and three cups of water. Allow it to boil several minutes before adding the suet. After the mixture cools (but before it jells) add rolled oats, chopped nuts, stale bread cubes, yellow cornmeal, and peanut butter (amount can vary). Roll the mixture into ball-shapes and package them individually in little squares cut from open-mesh sacks such as dry onions come in. Tie with a bit of bright ribbon and hang among the branches as you would on the family tree.

Hang crackers, stale cookies, and doughnuts, too. Fill favor cups with cracked corn, dry peas, or assorted nuts (unsalted) and suspend them here and there. Thread needles with colored yarn and string table variety cheeses, cranberries, and popcorn. Loop the tree with these nutritious chains and get ready for the birds' reaction.

Some birds like melons. If *your* birds are among them, cut melon rinds into chunks and include them on the menu. String dried currants and raisins and let the strands dangle for "easy picking."

Remember that some birds are salad lovers! For these birds no meal is complete without apple slices, banana wedges, whole plums, cabbage wedges, and lettuce leaves. Your guest list will grow as the menu varies.

Sprinkle rice on the ground to resemble snow (if you live in a warm climate); make it prepared cereal if nature sends snow on her own. Be generous with sunflower seed, acorns, and sesame seed in order to accommodate both large and small birds. And, last, would you believe that some birds like dog biscuits?

And remember that birds get thirsty even in winter. Place little tins of water here and there around the tree. In cold climates, you will need to change it often if the temperature is low.

A custom revived can add to your Christmas pleasure this year. Think of the fun you and your family will have decorating the tree. But most important of all you may very well be saving the lives of many little songbirds who will reward you with their music, come Spring. What a wonderful way to say "Merry Christmas!" to God's little creatures.

June Masters Bacher

This Day

This Day won't come my way again,
So let me take the time,
To make another's holiday
As full of joy as mine.

This Day won't come my way again,
So let me freely share,
The blessings of the Season
With those for whom I care.

This Day won't come my way again,
So let me spread His love.
As God did when He sent His Son,
Christ Jesus from above.

Rosalyn Hart Finch

A Christmas Sampler Box

ONE of the joys of each Christmas season is all the home-made baked goodies and mouth-watering treats that come popping out of the oven of some creative homemaker. An even nicer surprise at Christmas is to receive thoughtful gifts of home-baked goodies from special friends.

Have you thought of a Christmas Sampler Box of seasonal treats with a little bit of this, and a little bit of that, to share with trusty friends? You don't have to pack a whole loaf of nut bread. Put two or three slices in a waxed sandwich bag, then wrap it in foil, and place it in that empty box which formerly held the cards you've now addressed and sent.

Next to the foil-covered sack, put three or four of your favorite sugar cookies covered with red and green sprinkles. Then add a piece of brown sugar fudge with a big half-walnut on top, or a piece of white divinity covered with coconut. Or try some candied orange peel or grapefruit peel.

These small seasonal treats add up to large quantities of pleasure and happiness for the receiver. They can be sent through the mail also. In fact, one of the most appreciated gifts I made one year was a dozen fruit cookies, mailed to an elderly couple in another state.

They wrote: "We are slower now in getting out our cards, and the sight of these lovely cookies somehow persuades us to keep on writing personal notes. It saved us a trip to the store, too, for it was a cold day and we didn't really want to go outside."

My gesture had been such a simple thing to do, but the results were rewarding. Why not try giving a Christmas Sampler Box this season to those who long to remember the fragrance of a home kitchen?

Ruth C. Ikerman

Thank You, God

We're coming to that time of year
That's filled with joy and love and cheer.
The gifts are wrapped, the wreaths are hung,
The trees are lit, the carols sung.
But midst our hurried rushed December,
Let's stop — let's remember:
That through a Baby's lowly birth,
God gave His greatest Gift to earth.
And we who in His name believe,
The gift of LIFE we have received.
With all the tasks we've got to do,
Let's take the time to say, "Thank You."

Donna Russell

Look-Ahead Gifts

WOULDN'T it be nice if we kept Christmas alive after the carolers have gone, the Nativity scenes packed away, and the eaves stripped of their colored lights? This year why not resolve to keep alive the essence of the season by putting some year-round Spirit into your giving. It can be done — with a generous outlook at the world and an appreciative heart to the thoughtfulness of others.

Here are some look-ahead gifts that show your loved ones you want them to remember the gift of giving long after the holidays are past:

1. Plant daffodil bulbs in clay pots. Include a card telling the recipient how to take care of them when they bloom.
2. Bake a chocolate cake for a shut-in. Tuck in several copies of your recipe in case the person wishes to share a slice and "how-to."
3. Volunteer several hours of yard work at weeding time to a family member, a new neighbor, or a friend who shares flowers or vegetables in season.
4. Treat Dad to a free car wash on specified Saturdays.
5. Plan an old-fashioned "living room picnic" at least twice during the year (specify the dates for your family).
6. Treat Granddad to a baseball game — take along horehound and licorice and promise (yourself) to listen as he reminisces.
7. Let your children "sleep out" in the living room now and then. Supply sleeping bags and fill a thermos with hot chocolate. And let them giggle all night long.
8. Give your wife an umbrella — and offer to take a walk in the rain with her.
9. Volunteer a service you have never done — maybe never even attempted — for your church or community.
10. Give a large-print Bible to a visually-handicapped person and volunteer to take turns reading aloud.

Now, think up your own — but remember: Save the greatest gift of all for yourself. Add an "I love You" to every note and every farewell. You'll have your reward!

June Masters Bacher

A Lasting Christmas

I keep a part of Christmas
For it helps to add a glow,
To the January darkness
And the February snow.
If March is cold and blustery
And though April brings us rain,
The peace and warmth of Christmas
With its happiness remain…

There's a beauty when it's Christmas
All the world is different then,
There's no place for petty hatred
In the hearts and minds of men.
That is why my heart is happy
And my mind can hold a dream,
For I keep a part of Christmas
With its peace and joy supreme.

Garnett Ann Schultz

Treasures from the Spirit

A Fireside Reader

The Land Between The Rivers
A Christmas Legend

by Arthur Gordon

LONG ago, when the rivers of America were still silver, two of them flowed — not far apart — into the great sea. Later they would be called the Ogeechee and the Altamaha; but in those days they were nameless because there was no one to name them. No men, no women. Just the animals and birds, the trees and shrubs, and of course the wind, which was fickle and fey, but also very wise.

One cold gray twilight when the days were short, the wind spoke to the animals and the birds that lived in the land between the rivers, and to the trees and the shrubs.

"Tonight," the wind whispered, "you must stay awake, and watch, and wait, because a great happening may come upon you. What or where it will be I cannot say, because I am only the wind. But there will be a sign; this I know. And when you see it, you should rejoice and be thankful, because this night nothing will be the same. Stay awake, then, and be ready."

The wind sighed away into the great live oaks and across the amber marshes, and the twilight deepened, and the stars came out. The animals and the birds and the trees and the shrubs took counsel together. Most of them were doubtful, some downright scornful.

"Who can believe what is whispered by the wind?" they said. And one by one they fell asleep, the deer and the foxes, the squirrels and the shaggy bears in the swamps. Even night wanderers like the raccoons and the opossums sought their dens. The voices of the birds were stilled. They closed their bright eyes and slept. All except one small brown bird who was troubled in his heart.

"Someone must stay awake," he said to himself, "and be ready to rejoice and give thanks if this marvel does come to pass. I will wait and watch." He sought a bush or tree to perch in, but none of them wanted him.

"We have your kind all day," they grumbled. "We need our rest at night."

But one tall green shrub took pity on the bird. "Here," it said, "I don't mind. Perch on one of my branches, and I'll stay awake and watch with you." So the forest slept, and everything in it except the small brown bird perched in the tall bush, waiting.

And near midnight suddenly a golden light appeared in the sky, like a mighty star, only much bigger, much brighter. Silently it moved across the astonished heavens, and the bird and the bush watched it until it disappeared over the rim of the world.

"Ah," they said to each other, "did you see that? How wonderful it was! We really should rejoice." So the bird sang and the bush rustled its glossy leaves, and they gave thanks and praise in this fashion until the stars turned pale and the sun rose out of the sea.

Then all the creatures in the forest were amazed, because everywhere among the branches of the tall bush were crimson blossoms, glowing like rubies amidst the emerald leaves. And on the topmost twig perched a bird of flame, still singing, its scarlet plumage brighter than the sunrise.

And the wind came again and whispered to all the creatures, "See, this is the reward of faith and hope and constancy." To the bush it murmured, "Green is the color of life and red is the color of sacrifice. Wear these hues forever." And to the bird: "Scarlet stands for the trumpet-sound of courage, and for steadfastness. Wear this badge until time is no more."

So it was, and so it still is. We call the bush the camellia, now, and the bird the cardinal. But what we call them doesn't matter, they are what they are.

This is the story they tell to this day in the Georgia low-country where I was born. They tell it every year, yes, every year when Christmas draws near. And some of us believe it may be true.

The Crooked Dogwood Tree

by Peggy Brooke

All day the rain had drizzled down. Now, as evening fell on the little hillside, a harsh wind chilled the wet trees.

The little dogwood tree shivered in the cold. All was lost for him. That morning the village carpenter had come to the woodlot in spite of the rain to select trees to make into beautiful furniture for his wealthy customers.

He had snorted in disgust when he saw the crooked little dogwood.

"Cut this tree down for firewood tomorrow when you clean out the woodlot," he ordered his helper.

The little dogwood could hear the branches of the other trees rustling in the winds. "We told you so," they hissed.

The little dogwood's crooked trunk cowered in shame. He hardly noticed which trees the carpenter selected for his fine furniture.

The next morning the carpenter's helper cut down the crooked dogwood along with the underbrush and loaded them on a cart.

"Fit only for firewood, only for firewood," the wind seemed to whisper. How cruel life seemed to the little dogwood. The sooner the fire devoured his crooked limbs, the better it would be.

But that afternoon when the carpenter's helper unloaded his wagon, he paused and looked thoughtfully at the little dogwood.

"This should do for old Bossie," he chuckled to himself.

He lifted the little dogwood out of the wagon and began sawing and hewing the crooked trunk and limbs. Then, whistling to himself, he fitted and hammered the rough-hewn pieces together.

In the evening, the carpenter's helper tossed the newly-shaped dogwood into his wagon and rode to a neighbor's house.

"Ho, ho, Reben! What have you brought me?" a deep voice called out.

"Only a manger for old Bossie," the carpenter's helper replied.

"Ah!" the older man chuckled as he lifted the newly-formed dogwood out of the wagon bed. "It's crooked and surely not made of fine-grained wood. But it will do to keep Bossie's hay dry and out of the dung on the stable floor!"

The dogwood was carried into a shadowy stable and his new-shaped arms were loaded with hay.

Later that night, Bossie plodded faithfully into the stable at milking time. She chewed noisily on the hay as she leaned over her new manger. Then she rubbed her neck against the rough dogwood sides.

"Well," sighed the dogwood, "I guess being a manger is no more honorable than being firewood — a lowly occupation reserved only for the crooked and ugly." He felt so sorry for himself — so good-for-nothing. He could not forget what a fine piece of furniture he could have made if only he had grown up straight and tall.

Suddenly the quiet in the stable was broken by the sound of footsteps. A man trudged silently inside. He tied a small donkey just inside the door and helped a young woman slide from the donkey's back. She sank gratefully into the soft straw on the floor of the stable.

There was a strange sensation radiating from these two people. Being so close to them, the little dogwood felt his self-pity lifting and in its place a warm glow of peace and contentment was forming.

The feeling grew through all the unusual events of the night...the birth of a baby, the singing of angels. The little manger watched in awe as the lovely mother wrapped her baby in swaddling clothes. Then she paused, looking questioningly at her strong, silent, husband.

Suddenly the little dogwood manger felt himself being lifted. The husband placed the manger in the center of the room near where the young mother rested.

Gently she smoothed the hay in the manger, hollowing a little nest. There she lay her baby.

At the touch of the warm little body nestled in his rough manger arms, the dogwood manger thought he would burst with happiness. For something in the angels' songs told him that he was cradling a king!

His little heart throbbing with love and joy, he knew at last that he would never again be ashamed of his crookedness or ugliness. For he was being used to cradle the King of kings — the purpose God had in mind for him when He lovingly made the little dogwood unfit for anything but a manger.

My Very Special Christmas Tree

by Madeline Weatherford

CHRISTMAS was the most special holiday of all for my father. The preparations, gift buying and decorations were no trouble to him and just added to his overall enjoyment.

I was introduced to my first Christmas tree when I was nine days old. Mother told me that it was a small tree but every ornament, candle and piece of silver tinsel were meticulously hung in place, as only he could do it. When he had finished, he took me from my bassinet and held me up to see his handiwork.

There were to be just four more of Daddy's Christmas trees — each one a little larger than the year before. And, of course, as I grew older his delight in Christmas rubbed off on me and it became my favorite holiday, too.

However, this year was going to be different. A short bout with pneumonia in February had snuffed out Daddy's life.

As Christmas drew near, Mother sat down with me and as gently as she could explained, "Madeline, we won't be able to have a tree and decorations this year because we're in mourning."

"In mourning" meant nothing to a four-going-on-five year old little girl. I missed my wonderful daddy and my once gay and beautiful mother, now weighed down by her grief.

Christmas Eve arrived with no special arrangements for the next day, other than early Mass and dinner with relatives. In the afternoon the phone rang and Mother answered.

"Oh, hello, Mrs. Dreyfus," she said. And after a pause, "That's very kind but I think we'll spend the evening here together. It's the first since — " She recovered and thanked Mrs. Dreyfus again and hung up.

Mrs. Dreyfus was one of several Jewish families who lived in our apartment house. They had been wonderful to mother in helping her meet her sorrow and adjust to widowhood.

"What did she want?" I asked.

"She wanted us to come down this evening. I — I can't."

"Oh, please, Mother," I cried. "She always has hot cocoa for me."

Mother was silent most of the day and later in the evening she changed her mind. She called Mrs. Dreyfus and told her we'd stop in for a few minutes. "It's kind of her," Mother said, "and thank goodness they won't have any Christmas decorations."

We rang the doorbell and Mrs. Dreyfus welcomed us into the foyer. The living room beyond seemed dark with an odd-colored glow.

She led us into the living room where we were greeted with cries of "Merry Christmas." Seated around a beautifully decorated Christmas tree were Mrs. Abrams, Mrs. Cohen, Mrs. Blount. Under the tree were gaily decorated packages for us. And Mrs. Dreyfus didn't disappoint me. There was cocoa for me and coffee for the ladies.

There have been many, many trees since then — big, small, fresh and artificial — but I always think of that one as my very special Christmas tree. I'll never forget those loving, caring people who shared in an unfamiliar custom so that one little girl without a Daddy could have a Merry Christmas.

Today I can close my eyes and bring back that scene at will. Many times it has sustained me when things have gone badly; for I can still feel the warmth and love of those neighbors. It taught me the true meaning of Christmas — the brotherhood of man.

The Tie Clip

by Dick Schneider

IT was the day after Christmas, 1932, and a blustery wind traced white veins of snow across the sidewalk in front of our house. I glanced out the window of our living room where I was playing with my Christmas toys and the joy of the moment was snuffed as quickly as a candle.

Uncle Emil was coming.

A black sheep in the family, he worked on and off for the Chicago and North Western Railroad. He held the job only because he had lost an arm as a youngster while ducking between some freight cars, and the railroad felt it owed him this much.

However, the loss never seemed to bother Uncle Emil. Often, when his heavy jowls were flushed, he would take a stance like an angry bull elephant in the middle of the living room and boast of how many men he had fought to the ground with his one good arm. Every once in a while he would disappear into the bathroom and reappear ruddier than ever. It took me a few years to realize that it wasn't his kidneys but a pocket flask that prompted these frequent visits.

He had been married once, or twice; no one really knew. And now he lived alone in a room on Chicago's west side.

Uncle Emil talked incessantly of things of no interest to a ten-year-old; of ways to win at the race track, important positions he had turned down at the railroad, and, after several trips to the bathroom, of new speakeasies he had found. Bored almost to sleep, I listened with half an ear only.

One unforgettable year when his voice reached a high intensity, he became quite enthused about a new set of false teeth. Suddenly he took them out and flung them across the room for me to inspect. Trying to hide my disgust, I gingerly handed them back and ate little dinner afterwards.

Thus, every December as the holiday approached, I would complain to my mother about Uncle Emil's impending visit. "But why, Mom, why?"

"Because it is Christmas."

"He *ruins* Christmas."

"He has nowhere else to go," said Mother, her mouth firm, signaling an end to the discussion.

And now Uncle Emil was coming. Two days ago, Mother had given me a dollar to buy a gift for him.

As I entered the five-and-ten, a seed of evil entered my soul. Looking at the worn dollar bill, I could see no reason why I should buy that man a gift when there were so many things I needed. There was a model of the Gee Bee Sportster airplane I had always wanted to build. It cost seventy-five cents, but I could still find something nice for Uncle Emil with the remaining quarter.

Finding something for twenty-five cents wasn't as simple as I had thought. But the salesgirls were beginning to drape clothes over the counters as closing time neared, and I settled on a cheap gold-colored tie clip.

I eased my conscience with the thought that,

after all, he never brought us a Christmas present. At least an aunt brought chocolate coins in gold foil though they tasted of moth balls from a year's storage in her dresser drawer. She always bought her holiday gifts at after-Christmas markdowns.

Uncle Emil settled himself in his usual chair, and again I sat through the usual harangue, interspersed with bathroom breaks.

I had not shown Mother his gift. I wrapped it beforehand and presented it to Uncle Emil in the living room while she added last-minute touches to the dessert.

Just as he unwrapped it, Mother stepped into the living room. One glance at the tie clip and she turned to me, eyes blazing. Then, quickly covering her anger, she said: "Come, Emil, it's time for dinner."

Heaving his ponderous bulk from the cushioned chair, he slipped the tie clip into a coat pocket and lumbered to the table.

After dinner, Mother helped him into his coat and then stood at the living room window watching him walk, head bent into the swirling snow, to catch the streetcar.

Retribution rained heavily on me that night. Mother informed me in no uncertain terms that Uncle Emil never wore ties because he couldn't knot them. And, if I had any thought for others, I could see that.

The following spring Uncle Emil died. After the funeral, Mother and I went to clean out his room, a small, dingy chamber that smelled of mouthwash and shaving soap, with a cracked green shade at the window. It was the first time that I saw where he lived.

While Mother packed clothes into a carton for the Salvation Army I studied the walls of his room. Cracked yellowing snapshots were stuck inside the frame of his mirror; here and there an old letter, wrapped in a ribbon. Treasured fragments of those he had loved. And then something caught my eye. I couldn't believe it. Up on the wall, clipped on a Christmas card from our family was the cheap tie clip, tarnished by the past four months.

On the card with it were some words in his labored scrawl. I stood on tiptoes and dimly made them out:

"Christmas, 1932, from my nephew."

Suddenly, Uncle Emil's life fell in on me — his losing battle with the world, his hunger for companionship, his longing to have someone with whom to talk.

The shadowed glint of the tie clip wavered and dimmed in my vision. Wiping my eyes, I moved over to Mother, stumbling gently into her side.

"Mom," I said over a lump swelling in my throat, "I'm awfully glad we had him for Christmas."

She glanced up at the tie clip, and then at me. She reached down and gripped my shoulder for a moment. I think she knew that in Uncle Emil's room I had begun to grow up.

A Tradition All Her Own

by Frances E. Wilson

CAREFULLY she placed the small figure of the Christ Child in the crèche. For seventeen years, setting up the crèche just before Christmas had been her special tradition. As she stood back to admire it, she recalled the year it came to her. Yes, came to her with warmth and love.

She was ten years old that first Christmas of the crèche. It was just two weeks before the big day and all the houses on Mulberry Street were decorated with wreaths of green fir and bright red ribbons.

Pamela started counting them as she walked home through the powdery snow that had frosted the town white the night before. She noticed that even old Mrs. Kessel had hung a wreath on her door. It must have taken a lot of effort, Pamela thought, for she was badly crippled with arthritis and could barely get about.

Pamela lifted her feet in high steps and continued marching along. She made a path of big holes as she pushed her feet squarely down into the drifts of fresh snow. She hoped it would snow some more. You need to have snow for Christmas, she thought. Just like you need to have those Christmas customs her teacher had talked about at school that day. Miss Snyder had told the class about the special things people did to celebrate the holidays: putting lights and tinsel on the Christmas tree, wreaths of pine cones, hanging stockings, caroling. Pamela did wish, however, that she had something special she could do at Christmas, a custom all her very own. She thought about that as she walked the rest of the way home.

Once inside the warm house, Pamela hung up her coat and hurried into the kitchen where her mother was chopping nuts and measuring candied fruits for fruitcakes. Pam took a round, red apple from a bowl on the kitchen counter and bit into it. She watched her mother pour the nuts and fruits into a glass mixing bowl.

"Mother, you always make fruitcakes for Christmas, don't you?" she asked, her elbows propped on the counter top, her eyes studying her mother.

"Yes, I guess you'd say that," her mother answered, stirring the mixture with a wooden spoon. "In fact, fruitcake and floating island pudding are holiday traditions I've known since I was a girl, even younger than you. Some time you could learn to make it, then you'd be carrying on a family tradition."

"I guess so," Pam sighed, tossing her apple core in the trash bin. "What I'd really like though, is a tradition all my own. Dad always picks out the Christmas tree for us and sets it up in the tree stand. Tommy always puts the lights on the tree because he's tall enough to reach all the branches. Why, even Annie gets to place the silver spire on the top of the tree and she's just a baby!" Pam sighed and pushed her brown hair back behind her ears.

Her mother put her arm around Pam's shoulders and gave her a quick hug. "Your daddy used to hold you up to put the silver ornament on top of the tree. Don't you remember that? That's always been the special job for the youngest member of the family."

"That's just it! Everybody in our family has something special to do for Christmas!" Pam bit the corner of her lip. "Everybody but me!"

"You could string cranberries and popcorn to hang on the tree," her mother said.

"That would be O.K. for one time, I guess," Pam said with a shrug. "But I want something more," she narrowed her eyes thoughtfully. "I want something that could really make Christmas special for me, too — every year."

The next day after school Pam walked with slow steps toward home. Her head bent down, she shuffled her feet through the snow. "I just don't feel much like celebrating Christmas this year," she said half aloud. As she reached down to scoop up a handful of snow, she caught sight of a folded newspaper sunk in a pillow of snow at the edge of Mrs. Kessel's yard.

Grabbing the paper, she hurried up the walk and rang the doorbell. She brushed the snow from the paper with her mittens as she waited. She knew it would take Mrs. Kessel a while to answer the door for she walked very slowly using a cane.

"Pamela, my dear," the grey-haired lady greeted her with a smile of welcome. "My newspaper, how nice of you, dear. Won't you come in and visit with me? It's too cold to stand out there." She smiled at Pamela.

Entering Mrs. Kessel's living room, Pam stuffed her mittens in her coat pocket and took a seat on the couch near Mrs. Kessel's rocking chair. She did like visiting Mrs. Kessel. She was always so friendly and everyone in the neighborhood liked to listen to her stories. And she was a good listener, too. Pam found she was soon telling Mrs. Kessel all about her wish to have a special Christmas custom, telling her about Mother's special pudding and how Anne was the one who put the top spire on the tree.

"You know, Pam, I believe I have something put away that will interest you," Mrs. Kessel said as she leaned forward in her rocker and pointed toward the dining room. "Go open the right hand door of the buffet and bring me the white, cardboard box you'll find there."

In a minute Pam returned with box tied with white string. "What is it? What's in this box?" she asked. She was finding this an exciting mystery and her fingers trembled as she worked to untie the string.

"You'll soon see, dear," Mrs. Kessel said with a smile.

With a gentle yank, Pam had the cord free. Lifting the box lid, she discovered several packages wrapped in tissue paper.

"Take each of them out, one at a time," Mrs. Kessel instructed. "As you unwrap them you can set them in order here on the rug." She pointed to the space in front of her chair.

Pam had already begun pulling away the tissue. "Oh, what a darling little wooden lamb," she exclaimed as she put the small carved animal on the rug and reached again into the box.

Within a few minutes, she had four more sheep and three long-legged camels lined up on the carpet. She opened a larger package and discovered it contained several shepherds and also three kings. Pam knew they were kings, because they wore crowns on their heads.

"Why, these are the shepherds who took care of all the lambs and the kings who rode on their camels to see the Baby Jesus," Pam cried, her voice was filled with delight. "It's just like the manger scene in front of our church!"

"That's right, Pamela. It's called a crèche. At Christmas time in my home in Vienna my family always placed these nativity figures and the manger on the mantle above our fireplace."

"This was *your* special custom then, wasn't it?"

Mrs. Kessel nodded. "I haven't set it up for several years now. It is so difficult with my arthritis, you know."

"I'll set it up for you!" said Pamela excitedly. She placed the rustic crib on Mrs. Kessel's mantle and arranged the kings and the shepherds, Mary and Joseph. Carefully she took the tiny figure of the Christ Child and placed it gently in the crib.

"Thank you, my dear," said Mrs. Kessel. "But now I'm afraid you'll have to come back after Christmas and pack them away."

"Oh, I don't mind," said Pamela. "I'll do it very carefully. And next year...next year, I'll set them up for you again. I mean — could I, Mrs. Kessel?" Pamela ran to the woman and knelt at her feet, her face bright with anticipation.

"Yes, yes, Pamela, I'll look forward to it," said Mrs. Kessel. "Our little visits mean so much to me."

Suddenly Pamela struck her forehead with the

palm of her hand. "This is it," she cried. *"My very own Christmas tradition!"*

For five more years, Pamela set up and took down Mrs. Kessel's crèche at Christmas time, sharing with the elderly woman moments of peace, warmth and friendship. When Mrs. Kessel died, her will stipulated that the crèche should go to Pamela.

Now she stood in her living room, staring at the lovely figures with wonder that filled her every year at this time. As she touched them, her two-year-old toddled in from the playroom.

"What's that, Mommy?"

She picked him up and held him close. "That's Mommy's very own tradition," she said.

He looked puzzled. "Someday you'll understand," she murmured.

The Fourth Wise Man

by Linn Ann Huntington

LOOKING back, I can't recall exactly who thought up the idea for the practical joke on Richie. Maybe it was Jimmy Ray or Ben. Maybe I did. It was one week after our team, the Blue Raiders, had lost the 8th grade district football title. And there was no doubt in any of our minds as to whose fault that was — Richie's.

I don't know when I first realized Richie wasn't quite like everyone else. He was a year older than the rest of us, having been held back a grade. He was a big kid who walked awkwardly and spoke haltingly.

We were behind by three points when Richie came into that game. He broke through their defensive line with no trouble at all. Jimmy Ray lofted a perfect pass and Richie stood there in the middle of the field and pulled it in. The crowd went wild, screaming "Go, Go." And maybe that's why it happened. In all the noise, Richie became confused and ran the wrong way. It was a 46-yard touchdown pass and Richie had scored six points for the *other* team.

So that's how we came to think up the joke on Richie. Every year on the day before Christmas vacation our homeroom had a Christmas party in the afternoon and the traditional pageant for our families that night. We all drew names from a box and bought an inexpensive gift for that person to exchange at the party. I drew Richie's name and Jimmy Ray and Ben and I knew just what we'd get him. It was more expensive than the usual things but we pooled our money. The joke on big, slow Richie was worth it.

As we nibbled the cookies and sipped the punch the PTA provided, we could hardly wait for the gift opening. Finally our teacher, Mrs. Marlowe, announced that it was time for Santa's arrival. The principal, dressed in a Santa suit, came running in with a lot of "Ho, ho, ho's" and started picking up the packages under the tree and calling out the names. There were the usual scarves, records and other stuff that each kid knew the other had wanted. We knew Richie wanted the gift we had for him but he was in for a real surprise.

Finally Richie's name was called. I held my breath as he fumbled with the ribbons and paper. Then he pulled out a football. Ben had painted it a garish purple, intended to resemble our school color. The inscription in bold red letters said mockingly, "OUR HERO."

The cafeteria grew quiet. Mrs. Marlowe turned around, her face angry. Her eyes searched the room and rested on the three of us. I was trying hard to keep a straight face but in that instant I knew *she* knew. And I also knew we were in for big trouble.

Richie just stood there in the middle of the room, his mouth open. He gently stroked the football, his eyes blinking behind thick glasses.

I tried to duck out of school as soon as the party was over, but Mrs. Marlowe stopped me. "I want to talk to you, Carl. Why did you do it?"

"It was just a joke," I mumbled, wishing I could fall through the floor.

"A joke!" She paused. "We'll talk about this later. I don't have time right now, but I want to see you backstage after tonight's program. Understood?" I nodded.

The Christmas pageant helped take my mind off my own problems. The Glee Club sang Christmas carols during the set changes, the candles they held flickering softly in the auditorium. From the elevated cage where I worked the lights I had a good view of the stage. Now my spotlight focused on one single large star near the top of the backdrop. I could almost visualize how it must have been on that night long ago, how vast the sky must have looked to those shepherds tending their flocks outside Bethlehem.

Then the narrator's voice was saying, "And suddenly there was with the angel a multitude of the Heavenly host, praising God and saying, 'Glory to God in the highest, and on earth peace, good will toward men.'"

Good will toward men. The words made me wince. Mrs. Marlowe's eye caught mine and I wished I'd never seen or heard of that stupid football.

I asked one of the other guys to take over for me and I hurried toward the dressing rooms. I found Richie sitting alone in one corner, dressed as a wise man, the football in his hands.

I stood before him, hands sunk in my pockets and took a deep breath. "Richie, I'm sorry. I was the one who gave you the football."

He looked up. "*You* gave me the football, Carl?" I nodded, my face feeling flushed. "It must have been awfully expensive, Carl. I always wanted a football. You're a good guy, Carl." Richie's face lit up and he smiled a wide smile at me.

I started to speak but suddenly he heard his cue and he hurried up to the stage. From the wings, I watched the three Wise Men make their way on stage. The first two in turn presented their gifts of gold and frankinscense. Then it was Richie's turn. Carefully he stepped to the manger.

"This gift I bring to the baby Jesus," he began. Then he paused. The crowd stirred uneasily. "This gift I bring to the baby Jesus," he began again. And from the folds of his robe he withdrew the gift. But it wasn't the expected flask of myrrh. I gasped along with the audience as Richie held up his purple football.

"I've always wanted a football of my very own," he said quietly to the doll inside the manger. "My friend Carl got me this one." He looked out to the audience. "This football means a lot to me," he stammered. "But I want to give it to the Baby Jesus." Gently he laid the ball in the manger.

The auditorium was silent as the curtain closed. Then the audience exploded into applause. Richie came up to me, his fake beard slightly askew. "You don't mind that I gave the football away, do you Carl?"

I shook my head, trying to dislodge the lump in my throat.

"Carl, those words on the football. What did

that one word say — H-E-R-O. What does that mean?"

I struggled to find the right words. "A hero is someone everybody looks up to."

He looked surprise. "Does everyone look up to me, Carl?"

I put my hand to his shoulder, then helped him straighten his crooked beard. "Yes, Richie, tonight you're everyone's hero. Just listen to that crowd. They're applauding you."

He listened and his face broke into a wide grin. I pushed him on stage for his curtain call. Mrs. Marlowe came and stood beside me.

"I heard what you told Richie," she said, smiling at me. "I think he was probably the wisest of our three Wise Men tonight. But you know," she added, smiling at me." I think maybe now there's a fourth one."

The Donkey

by Van Varner

HE was not a handsome animal, this donkey. His ears were too long, his body too squat, and his flanks were scarred with the welts of many beatings. He was a common creature, his coat the color of dust, dingy, far from the ivory-white hues reserved, as Scripture said, for the mounts of royalty. Common he was, yet stolid, standing wearily in the cold stable, his muzzle deep in barley, the rich-wet sounds of munching loud in the darkness.

Someone came into the stable. There was a rush of activity. The donkey's ears pricked as he heard the voice of the man, his most recent owner, "Wake up," the man whispered to the lady as a tiny light burst through the darkness. "Bring the Baby. We must go now. Quickly."

The man came to him, and adjusted the rope that served as his halter. This was a good man. The best. No beatings from him. No whips. No kicks. No cries of "Stupid beast!" Over and over again during the three tiring days of travel from Galilee, the man had patted him. "Good fellow," he'd said as the donkey picked his way skillfully among the rocks on the rude trail. The man had been gentle, too, with the lady. She had been heavy with Child, then.

The man led the donkey out into the open air. The sun was just beginning to appear. The lady came out, bearing in her arms a small bundle that she held close and tight. "But where?" she asked the man, fearfully.

"South," said the man. "Egypt, if we can."

The lady drew near the donkey and as the man prepared to help her mount his back, the donkey saw the Child for the first time, and the Child the donkey. In one quick moment the Child reached out and touched the donkey's short, coarse mane. The donkey shivered.

The lady settled on the donkey's back. "Good fellow," said the man as he gave the donkey a pat. And then they were off, the man, the lady, the Child, the donkey.

The morning sun was brightening the earth now, and as its first rays fell upon the retreating figure of the old donkey, they seemed to shimmer. Something had happened to the animal, an extraordinary change. There was pride in the lift of his head; his hooves rose and fell in clean, sharp beats; and his coat — no longer was it the color of dust. Now the donkey's entire body was of a hue befitting a royal Passenger, the color of ivory.

Silent Night

by Nancy Schraffenberger

THEY had planned it for weeks, with care and concern.

Not a single loved person or Christmas amenity was missing from Frederick Bonnerman's house on the night of December 24th. The scene was as perfect as a stage setting. But the minute his wife Carrie rolled his chair into the middle of the living room, he felt more than ever like a great wooden puppet.

All of his children and their wives and husbands were there, along with every one of the grandchildren — from dark-haired Stephen, on the threshold of young manhood at age thirteen, to small Amy, the five-year-old, a Christmas bonbon in her rose-pink dress. The spicy tang of bayberry candles, burning applewood logs and pine scented the air. In the corner, a towering evergreen glowed with its multi-colored lights and ornaments. The sideboard was laid with a buffet service of the best silver and crystal, pastel china and snowy linen, and, nearby, a tea table held eggnog, mulled cider, miniature sandwiches and cookies.

The old man looked at it all stonily then shifted his large frame to a more militarily erect position. His blunt lionlike features were still handsome at seventy-three, and he was dressed in the same green velvet jacket he'd always worn just for the holidays. But this time, for him, it was a charade, not a celebration. He'd bristled with annoyance when Carrie pinned a badge of bright crimson holly berries on his lapel, as if he were some sort of grand marshal. But she'd only smiled and, as she did every Christmas, had given him the small pottery figure to hold. He rolled it back and forth as he cupped it in his good left hand, the chipped and blurred figure of a sleeping Baby.

Now, one by one, the members of Frederick Bonnerman's family began approaching him, their faces expectant. Christmas had always been such a special time and they clearly hoped that this painstakingly wrought celebration would cheer him. But he fended them off with an icy blue stare, chilling their soft greetings with his silence. He knew he was spoiling it for them. He couldn't help himself. And that was the crux of it.

The stroke a few months earlier had left his speech garbled and his muscles uncooperative. And now he couldn't take care of the necessary tasks, couldn't feed himself or dress or keep himself clean without help.

Frederick Bonnerman was not a complaining man and not a self-pitying one either. He was too proud for that; his life, all-told, had been too fortunate to be whining about a few latter-day physical defects. So when the numbness had taken over his body, he had invited it into his spirit as well.

Behind his chair, he could hear Amy's voice, "Why doesn't Grandpa like me to pet him anymore?" and her mother hushing her. "Grandpa's been very sick. He's just tired, honey."

His lips trembled, and he pressed them into a stern, straight line.

Trying to make the best of the evening, his oldest daughter, Emily, started to play some carols on the piano. The grownups and children clustered around her, singing softly, aware of the heavy silence from the center of the room. Carrie sat beside him, her warm hand resting on top of his cold one, her light, sweet voice distinct among the singers. He shifted impatiently in his chair and she leaned close. "It'll be time to start the Bible reading in a few minutes. You're not getting too tired, are you, Frederick?"

He shook his head curtly, his eyes turning to the low table in front of the fireplace. There lay the family's Christmas treasure — century-old, handmade clay figures arranged in the familiar crèche grouping, except for the Baby he held in his hand. After the older children had taken turns reading the nativity Scriptures, the youngest, Amy, would put the Child in the manger. Exactly at midnight. Exactly as the Bonnerman children had done for three generations.

The old man's eyes rested on the figures: Mary and Joseph, the Wise Men, a shepherd, an ox and a lamb — their colors muted with age, the shapes nicked and worn. Frederick Bonnerman's own grandfather, a farmer and amateur potter, had formed them, not with great skill, but with an appealing, primitive simplicity — the work of a grown-up molding clay with the joy and freedom of a child. Much cherished, carefully preserved, they'd been passed from father to son, father to son, and every Bonnerman child's understanding of Christmas began with these old figures. It seemed, to Frederick Bonnerman, these were the only precious things he had left to give his family.

The mantel clock chimed 11:30, its mellow belltones mingling with the last notes of "It Came Upon a Midnight Clear." Emily turned to her father from the piano bench, eyebrows questioning. He nodded. They would begin.

Slowly, everyone gathered around the table, with Frederick's wheelchair at one end. Stephen opened the Bible to the chapter marked with a faded blue satin ribbon. He cleared his throat and began to read in his boy's cracking tenor: "And it came to pass in those days, that there went out a decree from Caesar Augustus..."

Stephen handed the book to his sister and she to the next oldest child until each had read — except for Amy, who would take the Baby to the manger.

The clock was striking twelve times as she came toward Frederick, sturdy as a cub, her silky brown hair cut like a close-fitting cap around her small head. Her little round face wore a serious expression, but her eyes danced with excitement and pride as they gazed into her grandfather's. Tenderly she lifted the tiny Baby cupped in his hand, turned in a whirl of rose-pink ruffles and stepped away from him toward the manger on the table. Then it happened.

One of Amy's feet twisted and she tumbled down like a dropped ragdoll, her arms flinging out, the clay Baby falling on the slate hearth with a small tinkling sound, the awful sound of breaking.

Amy's face broke too. He saw the look of happiness shatter. She turned to him. Everyone did. And then Stephen's voice interrupted the frozen moment. "Oh, please, Grandpa, please don't be mad...because we can still keep Him, can't we?"

He looked at the sad faces surrounding him. They looked back. And saw.

Of course, Frederick Bonnerman could not speak. But words weren't necessary, for a great warmth was rising in him, like a sun, up from his feet through all of his body until his eyes shone with the brightness of it and the expression on his face was speech itself.

His face said that whatever Frederick Bonnerman could not do, he was still able to understand, comfort, love and forgive.

For the space of a breath no one moved, and then it seemed to Frederick Bonnerman that no one was *not* moving. Hands were picking Amy up and arms were enfolding her and other hands were carefully recovering the broken pieces of pottery. And arms, many arms, were around the old man's shoulders. And with his good left hand he was reaching out to Amy.

For Frederick Bonnerman and his family, the Christ Child had truly wholly come.

The Best Shine in Peru

by James McDermott

THE flight had been one of the roughest Malcolm Eldridge had ever experienced.

At another time he might have enjoyed a trip to Peru. He had visited Lima three years before to help set up a factory plant conveyor system, and now had been grudgingly sent down to repair it. "But it's December twenty-second," he had complained to his supervisor. "I'll miss Christmas completely."

"Our contract with the Peruvians said we'd send a man *immediately* if our system ever broke down, and you're the only man who can get it going again. That's why we pay you so well, remember?"

"Yes, sir." Malcolm Eldridge replied. Once out of the executive's office, he said, under his breath, "And a Merry Christmas to you, too, Scrooge!"

By the time he picked up his suitcase and cleared customs, the airport seemed strangely empty. The throngs had quickly dispersed into a clattering collection of ancient automobiles. He felt a tug at his sleeve and a high-pitched voice said, "Hotel Bol-ee-var?"

"Yes," he said, "Hotel Bolivar. Is there a taxi?"

"Bol-ee-var taxi here ten minutes. While wait I give shine? Best shine in Peru!"

Malcolm looked down at his tiny accoster. He had a mop of jet-black hair and sparkling dark brown eyes, and a look that was half plea, half hope. He had a small shoeshine box in tow.

"Sure."

The taxi was twenty minutes late, but the shoeshine boy was as good as his word. Malcolm's shoes gleamed.

It wasn't until he was in the taxi that he noticed his largest Peruvian bill — worth over $30 — was missing. It must have stuck to the bill — worth about sixty cents — that he had handed the shoeshine boy, telling him to keep the change. He had kept the change, all right.

He told the taxi driver to wait and dashed back to the terminal. But the shoeshine boy had vanished. Malcolm Eldridge looked ruefully at his feet. "The best shine in Peru," he said wearily, "worth just over thirty dollars. Welcome to Peru, sucker."

On Christmas Eve one of the plant managers took Malcolm home for a Peruvian-style Christmas. It was very noisy with unruly children squirming everywhere, and the adults drank too much wine and were rather more boisterous than he thought seemly at Christmastime.

The next morning — Christmas Day — Malcolm took a solitary walk to the sea and sat on a high stone wall watching the rollers crest in and smash on the grey rocks below.

"I must be the spirit of Christmas past," he mused to himself. "In my country they care so little about the birth of Christ that it means nothing to send me away from my family at this time. In this God-forsaken land, they drink wine, let the children run wild — it's just another fiesta. Or time to fleece a tourist…"

Two days later, his job completed, he was

checking in at the airline counter. A porter in a baggy uniform rushed over to him.

"Are you the American from Hotel Bol-ee-var?" the porter asked breathlessly.

Here we go again, Malcolm Eldridge thought. "Yes, I stayed at the Bolivar."

"Did Pepe shine the shoes?" the porter asked.

"Yes, he..."

"This from Pepe," the porter said quickly. He held out a gleaming beaten silver belt buckle. In its center the letter "A" had been crudely, but elaborately, engraved. "The father of Pepe dead. The family of Pepe poor. Pepe make Christmas with your money. Shoes for family of Pepe and cooking pot. Pepe say thank you for the money, but..." and saying this the porter shrugged.

"What is the letter 'A' for?" Malcolm asked, pointing to the engraving.

"Pepe not know your name. 'A' is for *amigo* — 'friend' in Spanish." The porter shrugged again. "Or if not friend Pepe say 'A' is for *Americano*."

"Can you give Pepe a message for me?" Malcolm asked.

"Surely, sir."

"Tell him that he makes me proud to be his friend. Say that because of him I have suddenly had my best Christmas ever — right here in your wonderful country. Tell him, even though he probably won't understand, that he has made me a generous man in spite of myself."

"Oh, yes, sir," the porter said. "Pepe, he understand."

"Yes," Malcolm said, almost to himself, "I guess I'm the one who didn't understand."

The First Gift Exchange

by June Masters Bacher

THE little grey bird was growing tired. This was his first flight south to escape the bitter cold and his untried wings were weary. Dare he rest again? Yielding to an earlier temptation to rest was the reason he became separated from the flock. "I must go on," he told himself, remembering his mother's teaching, "lest the star should set before I find my way."

Flying alone against the star-struck sky gave him time to ponder the vastness of the universe — so different from the security of his down-lined nest. Weren't there more stars than he remembered seeing through the branches of his first home? Why was the one he followed so brilliant? Why did some of the other birds he had seen along the way to Judaea have such beautiful songs while he had only a wee chirp? And why were some so brightly-feathered while neither his breast nor his wings were touched with color? "I wish," he told the ever-larger star, "that I were beautiful — I wish my wings were strong. Maybe I will never reach my destination."

Down, down went the star — and then it seemed to stop. Could this be a sign that he, too, was to descend? Even as he hesitated, the little bird saw movement below. With a chirp of joy, he dropped to the earth. There he crouched, resting and listening for familiar bird-voices. But the sounds he heard were unfamiliar: a comforting "Moo," a sleepy "Ba-a-a," and the soft "Coos" of some strange bird.

Hopping to the nearby building, he peered inside and there saw a strange sight in the glow of a low-burning fire. A tiny baby, wrapped only in loose garments, lay partly exposed in the manger while the mother slept on the hay and the father dozed near the fire.

He had heard fire was important to people. For with no wings they couldn't follow the sun as birds did. The man should be tending the fire. If it went out, wouldn't the baby be cold or die?

"Wake up! Wake up!" The little bird tried to rouse the father, first with a chirp and then with a little tug on his mantel with his beak. There was no response from the sleeping man, but a low cry from the baby. Maybe he was uncovered.

As the bird flew over the dying embers he felt their warmth and saw to his surprise that the movement of his own wings had fanned life back into them. And then he knew what he must do.

All night he flew back and forth, back and forth. The embers burned lower with each flight and sometimes it was necessary to fly very close to fan any life into them at all. Often he felt uncomfortably warm and knew he was dangerously near the fire. But one thought remained. He must keep it burning to keep the baby warm.

As the first fingers of dawn reached through the cracks of the crude building, the little bird realized that he was too exhausted to continue his vigil. With a sad chirp of despair, he fell wearily at the feet of the father.

The man stirred, and picked up the fallen bird. This little creature kept the fire going," he said. Joseph checked on the baby, cozy and warm, touched the cheek of his wife tenderly, and then warmed the bird with his cupped hands. When he felt a stir of life, Joseph put down a few crumbs from last night's meager meal and poured water from an earthen pitcher.

As the bird bent his head to drink, something wonderful happened to his small breast. It turned brick-red — and beautiful!

"Thank you and thank you!" the little robin tried to chirp, but it wasn't a chirp anymore. The sound Joseph and Mary heard as he spread his strong new wings was a song, a carol, that echoed long after he had disappeared in the heavens. "Peace on earth..." it seemed to be saying again to the shepherds in the hills.

The Magic Christmas Bell

by Wanda L. Jones

THE weather was clear and cold as nine-year-old Melody left the school Christmas Bazaar with her single purchase — a tiny Christmas bell.

"It's a magic Christmas bell," the woman had said, a note of hushed wonder in her voice.

Melody did not believe in magic any more than she believed in Santa Claus or the tooth fairy.

"Every time it rings, they say, it brings a Christmas blessing, if the owner has the magic of Christmas."

"How do I know if I have this magic?" Melody had questioned. "Maybe the bell wouldn't work for me."

"It would be well worth finding out, wouldn't it? After all, what greater good is there than to give blessings to others?"

Even if it was just a plain Christmas bell with no magic at all, it was pretty and had a pure, sweet tone. It looked quite festive pinned now to her coat. As she jumped a snow drift, the bell gave a merry tinkle.

"Well, hello, little Christmas spirit. You sound like Christmas itself coming down the street." Mr. Swenson, the baker, was shoveling snow from the front of his shop.

"Reminds me of a little bell that used to hang on our Christmas tree when my daughter was a little girl. Whenever a draft would tremble the branches, the little bell would tinkle, and my daughter would call out from her bed, 'Is it Santa Claus, Papa?'" The old man's face clouded. "That was a very long time ago. My daughter and her family live far away now. I will not see them this Christmas. But, here now. Won't you come inside the shop? I baked some Christmas cookies this morning."

Melody followed reluctantly, fearing that even a few minutes with this sad old man would only spoil the afternoon.

"They're almond cookies, my daughter's favorite," he went on as he put a plateful on the counter. "I don't know what I was thinking. Six dozen Christmas cookies on Christmas Eve, and the shop closed tomorrow! They will grow stale with only myself to eat them! Foolish old man." He wiped his eyes with the corner of his white apron.

In the warm, steamy bakery the two ate cookies, talked about Christmases past, and to Melody's surprise were soon laughing merrily. Mr. Swenson's eyes grew bright, and Melody knew he was no longer sad.

As she rose to go, Mr. Swenson put several more cookies into a bag. His wrinkled face broke into a smile.

"Such a blessing you have brought me today, little Christmas spirit! I was feeling sad and lonely, but I shouldn't have. I have so many happy things to think about and little friends like you to visit me. Perhaps I'll even decorate a Christmas tree tonight — with a little bell on it!" he added with a wink.

In spite of the cold, a warm feeling inside her persisted all the way down the block. Melody gave a little skip that set her Christmas bell to tinkling.

Suddenly she heard deep sobs. A little boy was sitting in the snow, his sled overturned. Melody bent over to help him up. The Christmas bell jingled merrily. The tear-streaked face looked up, and the red, swollen eyes fixed themselves on the bell.

Melody jingled the bell again with her finger. "Do you like my bell?" she asked, smiling. "It's a magic bell, you know."

The little boy's eyes grew round with wonder.

"Is it really magic?" he asked shyly.

"For sure," Melody said emphatically, taking his hand. "Come on. I'll walk you home. You mustn't cry on Christmas Eve. It's a happy day."

Four houses down, she left the little boy at his door.

"What kind of magic does it do?" he asked, still awed by the bell.

"It makes things disappear," she replied.

"Like what, for instance?"

"Well, your tears, for one thing. They're all gone."

The boy laughed, squeezed her hand, and disappeared inside.

"Well, little bell, if you don't work wonders! Even if it isn't real magic," Melody said aloud as she headed homeward again.

On the corner a man was standing motionless. Melody knew by the red-tipped cane he held that he was blind. As she made a turn to go around him, her little Christmas bell tinkled sweetly.

"Who's there?" he called out, tilting his head to one side.

"Only me," Melody answered timidly. She did not make a habit of talking to strangers.

"Come here, please," he pleaded. "I've been standing here for quite a long time waiting for someone to help me. You see, I've dropped something in the snow, and I fear I may have covered it up looking for it. Would you take a look? It is a brooch, a very special brooch, for my wife. I must find it."

Melody knelt and began to brush away the snow. She soon found the brooch and placed it in the grateful man's hands.

"How can I thank you? You have saved me from a very unhappy Christmas. It was a blessing you came along when you did."

Another Christmas blessing! thought Melody. She waited for the walk light and bounded across the intersection toward St. Luke's Church. Father Jackson stood on the steps.

"Father Jackson, could I ask you something?" Melody began.

"Of course, Melody," the priest answered, "What is it?"

"Just one question, Father. Is there...could there be magic in a Christmas bell?"

"Magic in a bell?" The priest looked puzzled.

Briefly she told him the woman's claim about the bell. "And it's happened three times on the way home," she said, detailing her encounters. "Three times it rang and three times someone got a blessing. The woman said it would happen if I had the magic of Christmas. Do I have it, Father Jackson?"

The priest's face softened. "You do, indeed, Melody. You gave three blessings, sure as the world."

"Then it's true? The bell is magic?"

"No, not the bell, little one. The 'magic,' as the woman told you truthfully, is in you. It's love. That's the magic of Christmas. When you give love to those you meet, you give blessings indeed."

Melody turned toward home, her steps picking up speed. She wanted to think about what Father Jackson had said, but not now. She was too excited, and she felt unusually happy.

She did not notice that the priest was still looking after her or that the tension of a too-busy Christmas was gone from his face. Neither did she hear his words that were swept away by the wind.

"Keep working that magic, little one, and you will discover the real blessing it brings — the happiness that comes to the heart of the one who gives love."

The Christmas Miracle

by Jean Bell Mosley

"WHAT I need," Matt muttered to himself, "is a big fat miracle." He chopped away with all his twelve-year-old strength at the cedar he'd chosen for the Christmas tree.

It was up to him this year, what with Mom in the hospital and Dad there visiting her this Christmas Eve.

"I don't even know where the trimmings are, let alone how to get any lights," Matt continued, laying out his problem to the cold snowy world.

The tree fell with a soft swish. If it weren't for his younger brother and sister he wouldn't even fool with a tree or worry about lights for it. All he wanted was for Mom to be better and come home.

Matt slung the tree over his shoulder and hurried home. There was still the milking to do and the feeding. There'd have to be some sort of supper for Lance and Lacy. It would be late before Dad got home from the hospital.

He wondered how the school Christmas program had gone that afternoon. He'd had to miss it in order to cut his tree.

He had some trouble getting the tree to stand up straight in the bucket of sand, but when it was done he placed it in front of a big window that overlooked the meadow. He wished he'd had time to find the baubles or make some. The kids were going to miss the promised lights but if he'd had some tinsel or paper chains maybe they wouldn't be so disappointed.

"Just one big fat miracle," Matt repeated. He closed the door to the front room and locked it. If he didn't let the kids see it until after dark, they wouldn't miss the decorations and tonight he might think of something.

After the milking, he threw down hay for the horse and fed the pig. Purple dusk was settling over the countryside. He could see a light on at the house and knew Lance and Lacy were home.

Glancing at the darkening sky he saw the evening star shining brightly and knew that soon the stars would be thick as daisies in a summer pasture. He wondered if that long-ago Bethlehem Star had looked like this one. Probably bigger and more shiny, he concluded.

"It was a miracle, I guess — that special Star. And we don't have such miracles any more," he told the chickens as he scattered their corn. "But *I* could sure use a great big fat one."

He removed his cap again, dusted it against his jeans and put it back on. It was a gesture he'd seen his Dad do lots of times. He didn't know why but, for him, it seemed to punctuate things — like a period indicating it was time to get on with something else.

After supper, when Lance and Lacy had helped tidy up, Matt got out the old Bible. Every year Dad did the reading, but he was man of the house now.

"And, lo, the angel of the Lord came upon them, and the glory of the Lord shone round about them and they were sore afraid," he read.

"How was it, Matt?" Lance demanded. "How did the angel come?"

"Well, I suppose he just came down out of the skies."

"Did you ever see anything like that, Matt?" Lance pressed.

"Naw, things like that don't happen anymore. It was sort of a — well, a miracle, I guess."

"Are we going to have a tree this year?" Lacy asked when he had put the Bible back on the shelf.

"We've got a tree," Matt replied, feeling proud. "And I'll let you have just one little peek tonight."

He opened the front room door and they tiptoed inside, closing the door behind them. The tree stood outlined against the window. Matt heard a quick intake of breath in the darkness and waited.

"Oh, Matt, the lights!" Lacy exclaimed, clapping her little hands. "The lights! The lights! They're beautiful."

"What lights?" Matt asked.

"Nobody else ever had lights like these!" There was joy, awe, reverence in Lacy's voice.

"Where's the lights?" young Lance demanded.

"Come down here," Lacy said, pulling both their heads down on a level with her own. "See, at the very top and at the end of each limb — a star!"

It was true. The tree, silhouetted against the window, was alive with stars. They twinkled and sparkled through the branches with a very special one at the top.

"Oh, Matt, you did it," Lacy exclaimed, hugging and showering her brothers with kisses. "I knew we'd have lights!"

"I didn't do it," Matt said roughly, over the peculiar lump in his throat. "It's — it's — well, you know what I said about miracles not happening any more? That just isn't so." He spoke slowly, feeling his way, something new happening inside him.

"It's just where you're looking at it from. That's it. That's what makes a miracle. It's just who's looking at it and where he's looking at it from."

He reached to remove his cap. It wasn't there. So he just smoothed his hair and smiled. It was time to get on with whatever came next, especially in a world where big fat miracles still happened.

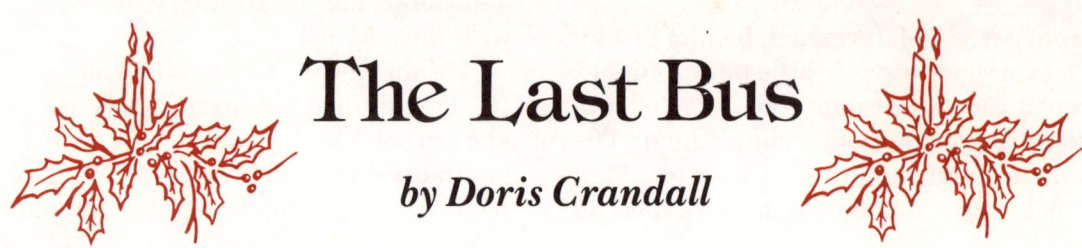

The Last Bus

by Doris Crandall

I REMEMBER the Christmas I decided not to go home. I was twenty-one, and living in Wichita, Kansas, far from my parents and the farm where I had grown up. I had only Christmas Day off from my job. I had been promoted to office manager just a month before. Determined to make good, I had worked to the point of exhaustion.

I'd welcome a day to myself. I'd attend a Christmas morning service, relax in the afternoon. If I went home I'd have to ride a Greyhound bus all night. I'd arrive in Shamrock, Texas, a small town nearest to the farm, at 6:00 a.m., and then in order to return to work the day after Christmas, I'd have to reverse the ride that night.

Not one to do things on the spur of the moment, I had sent Mama's and Daddy's gifts well ahead of time along with a letter saying how much I loved them and how much I missed them.

At that time, I could contact my parents only by mail. There was no telephone service to the farm, and Western Union didn't deliver messages to rural areas.

Having made the decision not to go home, I dug into my work and tried to forget that I wouldn't even be able to call my parents on Christmas Day.

At 5:30 on Christmas Eve, I wished my boss and co-workers a Merry Christmas and left the annual office party early.

On the way home I had to pass the Greyhound bus terminal. As I neared it, my steps slowed. When I saw the bus with "Oklahoma City" across the front, homesickness clutched my heart. I leaned against the building. *That's the last bus out to get me home by tomorrow morning*, I thought.

Woefully, I watched the passengers board the bus. The driver, taking tickets at the door, was one that I had ridden with several times before. When the last person got on, he looked my way.

"Hey, Sunshine, are you going or not?" he teased as he motioned and smiled.

My heart leaped. "I'm going," I said quickly. "Wait until I get a ticket."

Breathless, and tingling with happiness at the prospect of home, I settled into the only available seat. A short time later I wondered whatever had possessed me to make that snap decision. I hadn't even a change of clothing. And worse, since Mama and Daddy didn't know I was coming, how would I get the fifteen miles from Shamrock to the farm? I'd have to hitch-hike, but who would be driving down the country road at six o'clock on Christmas morning?

In the dim, early morning light, the bus pulled into the Shamrock station. About now, I thought, Mama and Daddy are in the kitchen. Mama has lit the gas cook stove and left the oven door open to help warm the room. They are having a cup of coffee before Daddy goes to the barn to milk the cows. While he's gone Mama will cook sausage, eggs, and hot biscuits with butter and syrup. It's Daddy's favorite breakfast.

As I stepped off the bus, a woman threw her arms around me and I was in Mama's arms. "How did you know to meet the bus?" I asked as I wiped the tears from my eyes. "I wrote you I wasn't coming home."

"The truth is," Mama admitted, "we both had strong feelings that you'd be on this bus. After all, it *is* the last bus before Christmas."

Then I told them about my irresistible and last minute urge to hop onto that bus. Had we unknowingly sent each other mental dispatches?

"No," Mama said thoughtfully, "I don't think so. I believe God just put it on our hearts. It's one of His Christmas miracles. Let's go home."

Of all my memories of Christmases spent with Mama and Daddy, the year that I was impelled to take the-last-bus-before-Christmas home is my favorite one.

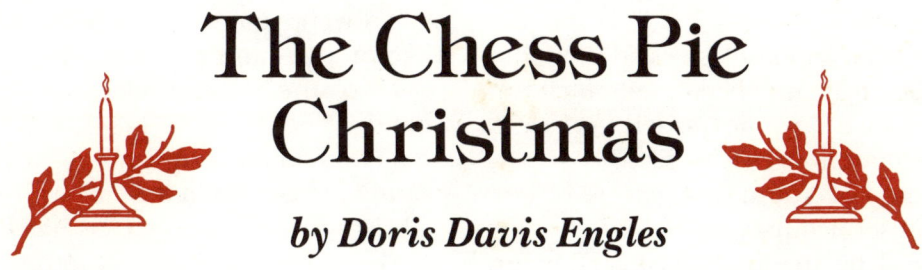

The Chess Pie Christmas

by Doris Davis Engles

IT wasn't my first depression Christmas, but it was the one that at age nine would forever change the way I believed Christmas should be. Our family was always together at Grandma's, but most of the preparations were complete by the time we arrived from Pittsburgh.

The one task left was the making of chess pies. These were individual pies that Grandma baked with extra love and care for our family and some of Grandma's special friends in the little town where she lived. So this was the Christmas event we always did together.

I watched as Grandma rolled out the dough.

"How many will we be giving away this year, Grandma?" I asked, wondering if I might have more than one for myself.

"Well, there's Uncle Zeke who lives alone, and the Evans sisters who have no other relatives to share Christmas with them. Then there's Aunt Emma who asks never to be left out of my Christmas pie list. Oh, yes, there's Mrs. Goldstein who's blind and lives alone. We mustn't ever forget her. You remember we went to see her last summer when you were here?"

I shivered as I thought about the dark old living room with its massive wall paintings and velvet sofa with claw feet that I felt might move at any moment. I hoped I wouldn't have to go there with the chess pies.

At last they were done. We would deliver them the afternoon before Christmas, but for now they must be put out of sight to be safe.

"Here, on the top shelf of this cupboard should be a safe place, and out of the way, too," she said. "I don't use it much."

The next afternoon we cleaned off the kitchen table to prepare the chess pies for delivery. Grandfather would drive us to Uncle Zeke's and Aunt Emma's. Then we'd go on to the Evans sisters' home where they would squeeze a nickel into my hand as we prepared to leave. Finally, near suppertime my job was to go to Mrs. Goldstein's since she lived the closest to Grandma's house.

The trays were on the table now ready to uncover. I couldn't wait to taste that brown sugary sauce, heavy with chopped nuts and raisins. I had decided to eat one of mine before we made our deliveries. Grandma peeled back the wax paper on the first tray and we both stared in amazement. She said nothing, but her shocked face was white.

"Oh Grandma, what's happened?" Bits of crust lay on the tray edges and there were holes in every pie. Quickly Grandma pulled the wax paper from the second tray. I felt relieved the minute I saw the pies. They were perfect. Nothing had bothered them.

"It must have been a mouse," she said thoughtfully. "That cupboard hasn't been used much for sometime. At least we have one tray left. As I see it we'll have just enough to give as gifts."

"Oh no, Grandma! You mean that we're not going to keep any for ourselves?"

"Dear, it would be so easy to keep them for ourselves. But Christmas means giving."

Why did that mouse spoil everything? All I wanted was one pie. Somehow this kind of giving wasn't what I'd expected of Christmas.

The disappointment I was feeling was still evident when I reached Mrs. Goldstein's big brick house with the huge windowed sunporch. I slipped inside and knocked at the inner door. It was dark and bare. No Christmas decorations appeared anywhere. Mrs. Goldstein opened the door just enough to ask who was there.

"I'm Doris, Mrs. Port's granddaughter," I mumbled. "I've brought you something for Christmas from my Grandmother."

"Come in, do come in, dear," she said loudly. She motioned me to a chair with her cane. I slipped into the seat covered with needlepoint and sat back in the cool dimness. My feet hung loosely above the soft carpeting, and I waited silently until Mrs. Goldstein seated herself nearby.

"Did you and your Grandmother bake those wonderful chess pies this year?" she asked smiling. "I always look forward to her thoughtfulness. It's really the only gift I'm given except from my family. And they're all gone from home now." I squirmed uneasily in the chair. She was going to have my chess pies.

"Yes, we made them yesterday. Grandma always waits until I come for Christmas before she bakes, because she knows how much I like them," I answered.

"Wait here," she said as she moved to the edge of her chair and then rose on her cane.

She tapped effortlessly across the room and disappeared through the hallway into the kitchen.

In a moment she returned, carrying a cardboard box lined with Christmas paper.

"This is for you, Doris. Since you delivered my gift, I want you to have this from me. I hope you like oranges and candy."

I took the box carefully from her outstretched hand.

"The fruit is from my son in Florida and the candy is from my daughter in New York. Merry Christmas and I know God has blessed you."

She was still smiling out into the darkness as I stepped on the sunporch and into the street beyond. Trudging along in the deeper snow I saw out of the growing darkness tiny new flakes drifting toward the ground. Lights in nearby houses were on now, and the brilliant color of Christmas trees flooded the windows. My fingers touched the edges of the wonderful candies under the paper covering, and I could smell the sweet fragrance of the oranges.

Somewhere down the block I heard sounds of Silent Night being sung by early carolers. Suddenly I knew the chess pies didn't matter. What mattered was having something to give.

Opening the door with one hand and waving the gift box with the other, I called excitedly, "Grandma, you'll never guess what happened!"

Chrissy's Shell Tree

by Velma Seawell Daniels

CHRISTMAS was only a week away that day I visited what I call "the shell tree."

I had driven down to our summer cottage at the beach to pick up a couple of books I needed for an article I was working on.

So, on this sunny December day, I slipped off my shoes and set out for a walk down the beach. "How good to be alive — and here," I said to myself, as the wind's playful fingers ruffled up my hair, and its salty perfume reminded me that it was clean and unpolluted.

Even my feet felt happy as they headed for the shell tree. It was at the lower end of the island, about a mile away, and I was curious to know if it was still there.

I had learned the true story of the shell tree from Chrissy Woolley, a dear friend and neighbor who told about it on her Christmas card one year.

"One day, after gathering shells for a collection for each of my children at school," she wrote, "I started for a long walk to the point of the island. Suddenly I was struck with the thought of gathering broken shells. Everyone gathers beautiful shells, but why not gather broken ones? I started picking up only the shells which were broken or had a hole in them. By the time I reached the point of the island, I had quite a collection. I noticed a bare weather-beaten tree at the edge of the mangrove, and the thought of decorating it with the broken shells came into my mind."

"What joy!" she continued. "While putting the shells on the tree, God showed me the message He was giving me. God has a place for broken things! He is the One who can ease our brokenness, heartache, defeat and discouragement and mold us to what He would have us to be."

As I walked on the beach, I thought about Chrissy's tree and what it meant. "I should look for a shell of some kind to add to it," I thought. So, I started searching for something suitable — obviously something broken. Several times I picked up one, only to discard it a few minutes later for one I liked better.

Then, when I was almost within sight of the tree, I saw what I was looking for. "It's just exactly what this old tree needs," I said aloud.

The tree was just as I remembered it. Some of the more recent additions were bright and colorful. Others had been bleached white by several years in the sun. Right at the top, a small dried up twig stuck out as though waiting for my gift to be added.

Stepping on the lowest branch of the tree, I placed my offering onto the twig.

I stepped back to look at my handiwork. A starfish — whole, not broken — crowned the tree.

"There you are," I said. "Today, instead of being just an old tree holding broken shells, you are a true Christmas tree standing on the beach to honor the Baby Jesus on His birthday. And this time one item is whole — The Star — because God is whole. Like the Star of Bethlehem, He is always looking down on the helpless and broken."

A Cold New York Christmas

by Dina Donohue

WHEN he ran away from home, Jon Tyler vowed he'd never think of Vermont or the stepfather who made his life so unhappy.

"He's too strict," Jon complained to his mother.

As always, she sided with her husband. "Bill is only doing what's best for you."

When Bill took Jon's driving privilege away for staying out too late one night and letting his school grades slip, Jon emptied his savings account and headed for New York City and independence. He sent a postcard home as soon as he found a job, telling his mother not to worry.

He had been in the city for two months now but he was still a stranger. People were cold and distant. The only ones he talked to were the other busboys at the fast food restaurant where he worked. He had a room at the "Y" but hadn't made any friends there.

It was his day off and one of the busboys had said, "You ought to see the tree in Rockefeller Center." He stood beneath the giant tree, sparkling with its tiny colored lights. He was surrounded by throngs of happy people, he watched the skaters on the rink below, he took in the decorations in the surrounding stores — and felt more lonely and miserable than ever. No one gave him a glance or a smile.

He shivered from the cold and headed for the warmth of a Fifth Avenue department store. It was a large store, but impersonal and distant despite the holiday decorations and Christmas music coming from overhead speakers.

People pushed past him, irritable clerks rang up sales. In Vermont, a customer would be greeted warmly by the owner of the store or the salesperson.

He walked through the aisles, amazed at the array of jewelry, scarves, purses and other gift items on display.

But he couldn't shake his desire to go home. It wasn't only the lack of fare money which gnawed at him. Maybe his mother and Bill wouldn't care if he didn't come back. Maybe they were happier without him.

It was just at this moment, with sudden tears clouding his eyes, that he bumped into a table piled high with leather wallets. Table, wallets and Jon crashed to the floor.

Stunned but not hurt, Jon lay outstretched on the floor until a security guard pulled him to his feet. He was half-carried to an office where a grim faced man sat behind a massive desk.

Questions came one after the other: had he been alone?...why did he knock over the table? ...would he voluntarily empty his pockets or should they call the police?...where were his friends?

"I just didn't look where I was going. I'm sorry," Jon protested. "I don't have any friends. I'm no thief." He willingly emptied his pockets.

The man behind the desk glared at him. "During the Christmas rush we have all sorts of people pulling tricks to steal merchandise. Crashing a table is one way to get attention away from a confederate staging a robbery nearby."

"No, I just came in to get warm. I was cold." And then, although he couldn't understand why he confided in this stern man, Jon said: "I bumped into the table because I was dreaming about going home to Vermont for Christmas. I ran away two months ago and I don't know if they want me back. Anyway, I have no money for fare."

The man's face softened. He reached for the telephone on his desk. "What's your home phone number, son?"

And a stranger in a cold, impersonal New York City store sent Jon Tyler home for Christmas where he was indeed wanted.

Since the first Christmas when a Son was the most welcomed of all babies, homecoming at Christmas has been a blessed and cherished tradition.

The Littlest Camel
by Shirley Climo

ST. FRANCIS of Assisi taught that all the gentle creatures that shared the stable with the Christ Child should share, too, in the anniversary of His birth. So, in many countries, it is a tradition to remember the furred and feathered members of the household at Christmas. In Scandinavia, sheaves of grain are tied atop the roof to feed the hungry birds. In Spain, extra rations are given the cattle in remembrance of the cow who warmed the baby Jesus with its breath. In Belgium, and in parts of France, lambs are brought to the church to be blessed on Christmas Eve.

According to Syrian legend, one animal present at that first Christmas was blessed in a special way. The three Wise Men had traveled many arduous miles upon their camels before they reached the stable. When, at last, the Magi dismounted to give the Christ Child their gifts, the first two camels also knelt and bowed their heads before Him. But the third camel, young and wearied from so long a journey, stumbled and sprawled beside the manger. The onlookers were horrified, and might have beaten the beast had not the Christ Child stayed them, lifting His small hand. He blessed the little camel and promised that henceforth it should be the bearer of gifts to all children in His name.

That is why children in Syria leave bundles of hay outside their doors on Three Kings Day (January 6). It is their thank you to "the Camel of Jesus," who, they believe, is still faithfully traveling the long miles to bring their Christmas gifts.

Bethann's Christmas Prayer

by Marilyn Morgan Helleberg

"PUT that doll down!" growled Mrs. Skorp, owner of Willow Creek's only store. "You'll break her!"

"Oh no," said Bethann. "I wouldn't hurt her. I *love* her!"

"Love her, do you? Well, you'd better get over *that* in a hurry." Mrs. Skorp whisked the doll out of Bethann's arms. "That's the most expensive doll in the store, and with your dad laid off..."

"It's o.k.," said Bethann, her wistful brown eyes skanning the drawn face of the middle-aged shopkeeper. "I won't touch her again until she's mine. She's my Christmas prayer!"

"Oh? I suppose you've been talking to Jesus again?"

"Why, yes! I have!" Bethann's pale, plain-looking face took on a sudden glow. "Last night, I talked to Him a long time — and when I went to sleep, an angel with golden wings floated down on a cloud and told me I could have one Christmas prayer answered this year. I could have anything I asked for — but only *one thing*. I've asked for Betsy."

"Betsy!"

"Yes, that's what I've named her."

Mrs. Skorp tossed her hands over her head and walked away. "Angels now!" she muttered.

By the time she got home, Bethann was near to tears. "I can't stand her, Mommie! Mrs. Skorp is the meanest lady in the whole world!"

"Don't be too hard on her, dear," said her mother. "Mrs. Skorp used to be a very nice lady...before the accident."

"The accident?"

"Yes. It was before you were born. The Skorps were driving home from Kansas City, after spending Christmas with relatives, when they hit a patch of ice and went off the road. Mr. Skorp was killed instantly, and their baby daughter died a couple of days later. Mrs. Skorp wasn't even hurt — at least, her *body* wasn't."

"I didn't even know she had a baby," said Bethann, fingering the hem of her skirt.

"After that, Mrs. Skorp just kind of dried up. She stopped going anywhere, closed herself off from everybody, even quit going to church. Some say she's been mad at God ever since."

"I've never heard of anyone being mad at God," said Bethann.

At bedtime, she knelt down and started talking with her Friend. "Lord, You know Mrs. Skorp — the one with the pinched up face and the screechy voice? You probably haven't heard from her lately because, well, I guess she's been mad at You for a long time. Anyway, Jesus, I've been thinking, and I've figured out a way to get her over being mad at You. So if You don't mind, I'd like to take back that Christmas prayer for my Betsy doll. Instead, Lord, would you please send Mrs. Skorp a new baby girl? Then maybe she won't be mad at you anymore. Thank You, Jesus."

After school the next day, Bethann stopped at

the store again, only this time, she was careful to not even *look* at Betsy.

"Mrs. Skorp, I talked to Jesus again last night..." The tall, gaunt lady grunted and turned away, but Bethann continued. "I asked Him to give you a new baby girl."

"You WHAT?!" said Mrs. Skorp, wheeling around. "You really *have* lost your senses! Besides, if there *is* a God, He sure doesn't answer prayers. Now you get on home!"

On the day before Christmas, Bethann made a paper card for Mrs. Skorp. The shopkeeper was alone in the store when Bethann tiptoed in. The woman was staring at a framed picture, clutching it so tightly Bethann saw that her knuckles were white.

"I brought you a Christmas card, Mrs. Skorp."

Surprised, the woman laid the picture on the counter and reached for the card.

She opened it and read the childish scrawl: "Jesus loves you. And so do I. Bethann."

Mrs. Skorp coughed and turned away. That was when Bethann sneaked a look at the picture on the counter. She saw a beautiful, smiling young woman, holding a curly haired baby in her arms.

"Is that your baby that died?" asked Bethann.

Mrs. Skorp slumped into the old library chair and put her head in her hands. "Her name was Betsy," she said.

Bethann stared at her.

The woman's body began to shake as deep, low sobs poured out of her. The little girl tiptoed over and put her hand timidly on Mrs. Skorp's knee.

"I asked Jesus to send you a new little girl to love," said Bethann. "Are you crying because He didn't answer my prayer?"

"No," said Mrs. Skorp. She scooped Bethann up into her lap, pressing the little head close to her heart and rocking back and forth, back and forth, in the straight chair.

"No, my little...darling. I'm crying because ...because He did."

Integrating the Family Treasures

by Ruth C. Ikerman

IT was the first Christmas since the marriage of my young friend to a handsome father of two children. Since he had their custody, my friend became an Instant Mother.

I asked her how the holidays had been, and a frown crossed her usually attractive face. "I'm so glad Christmas is over," she told me, "but next year will be better."

"What happened?" I asked.

"It was all because we had two boxes of decorations for the tree. My husband brought out the ornaments the children had used in other years. Jeff and Helen made a dash for their favorites, and immediately put them on the tree limbs."

Meanwhile, she told me, she had been unpacking the ornaments she had collected in ten years as a career girl, expecting the children to enjoy using them as tree trimmings. The children had no feeling for the crystal icicles, the fragile ornaments with little figurines embedded between the clear substances. They cared not at all for the figures made of straw which my friend had secured in her travels to foreign countries.

"It was a real blow to my ego," she told me. "I expected them to like what I had enjoyed so much. They didn't even want me to put them on the tree with their toy drums, soldiers, fairies and dollies.

"Finally I sat down on the couch with the children and told them stories about each of my treasures. I offered them a chance to each choose the ones which they liked best.

"Reluctantly the children peeked into the box, and Jeff took out some ivory animals I bought in Alaska. Helen chose a wooden manger scene carved in Italy.

"I told them these figurines were theirs to keep as long as they lived. Shyly they gave me their thanks at first, and then followed them up with real hugs.

"The tree looked a little lopsided and not as I had visualized it, but the longer I looked at it, the prettier their earlier ornaments looked to me. By the time Christmas was over it began to seem like a tree which belonged to all of us."

Wisely the Instant Mother had found one large box in which to put all the ornaments from the first tree they had shared.

"Next year we will just open one box together," she told me.

I patted her on the shoulder and told her how much I admired her wisdom and her courage. By integrating the ornamental treasures, she had made unity out of what might have become a divided Christmas.

Wise in the ways of love and Christmas was my young friend, and rich in memories will be the children and their father in the newly established loving family circle.

The Christmas Eve I Smelled the Hay

by Marjorie Holmes

CHRISTMAS EVE and we were late, as usual, herding our family into the hushed candlelit church. The last bell had stopped ringing; every seat was taken. The usher had to lead us up a side aisle to some steps where we could perch behind the choir loft, so close to the manger scene we could smell the hay.

Real hay...its pungent scent transporting me back to the sweet smelling hayfields of my childhood. The barns, the mangers. Suddenly I was shaken by a vivid sense of reality. For the first time in my life I realized, "Why, this *really happened*! There actually *was* a girl who had a baby far from home — in a manger, on the hay." A very young girl, probably — because I had recently heard or read that in the culture of Mary's time a girl was betrothed as soon as she went into her womanhood, and married before the year was out.

My own daughter Melanie, thirteen, who had just matured, was sitting beside me. And I thought, astonished, "Why, Mary couldn't have been much older than Melanie — perhaps fourteen — when she bore the Christ Child!"

With this awareness came a thrilling conviction about Joseph. He must have been a young man too; old enough to protect and care for her and the child, but young enough to be deeply in love with Mary. And she with him! Why not? They were betrothed to be married. Surely God, who loved us enough to send his precious Son into the world, would want that child to be raised in a home of love. A place where there was genuine human love between the two who were chosen to be His earthly parents.

I left the church in a state of great excitement. I knew I must write their story. I must make this blessed event as real for other people as it had become for me. That's when I thought of writing *Two From Galilee*. That wonderful Christmas Eve when I smelled the hay.

The Christmas That Changed a Town's Name

by Martin Buxbaum

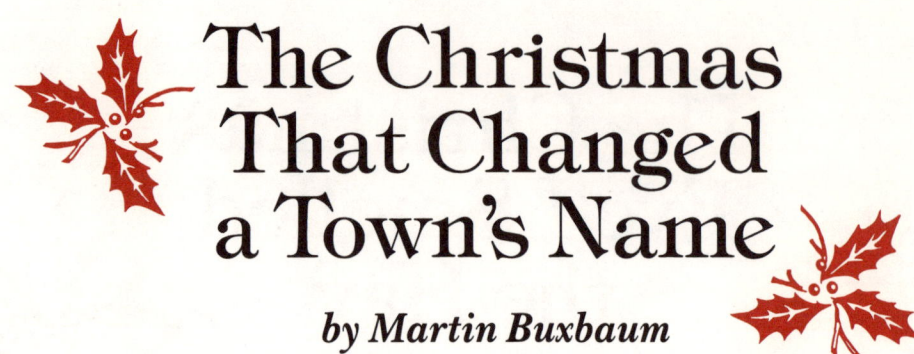

RIVER FORK was a small town, a friendly town, except for the Fletchers and the McCloskeys. They hadn't spoken to each other for two generations. No one seemed to know why they hated each other, not even the Fletchers and the McCloskeys. But the Fletchers did not speak to the McCloskeys and the McCloskeys did not speak to the Fletchers.

One night shortly before one Christmas something happened to change that and anyone who was there will tell you what made the citizens of River Fork also change their town's name.

It all began one November morning when plump, motherly, Mrs. Parris happily made an announcement to her fifth grade class: "This coming Christmas, children, our class has been selected to give a Christmas Play! We will begin choosing those who will play various parts and everyone will have *some* part in the play." Upon hearing this, the children clapped and squealed.

And so the players were selected and each child who had a speaking part was given a simple script.

The sixth graders were given the job of making the stage scenery. The seventh graders would play the music and parents would, as usual, be asked to make the costumes and provide refreshments. Mrs. Parris was determined to make this the best Christmas play the school had ever put on.

The list went on...Mr. Loveliss had agreed to lend a small, gentle burro and Mr. Baker promised to provide straw for the stable from his grain and feed store. One thing bothered Mrs. Parris, however — the infant Jesus. In almost all Nativity plays, a doll was used in the manger. But Mrs. Parris wanted it to be really special...the infant should be a real child. But who would lend a new baby for the school play? She decided to ask her students what *they* thought. She'd learned long ago that children were smarter than grown-ups believed they were — especially if given the opportunity to express themselves.

She asked her class what *they* thought of her idea of a live baby for the play, and the children all agreed — they wanted a real baby to be in the manger. That settled it. So next she asked if anyone had a baby brother. Only one hand was raised. It was Amanda Fletcher. "Yes, Amanda? Do *you* have a small baby brother?"

"No, ma'am, but I have a baby sister. She's three months old and she never cries."

Aaron McCloskey snorted. "Jesus wasn't a girl. That's dumb. A girl for the Baby Jesus!"

"Now wait a moment, children," said Mrs. Parris. "The baby will be in a manger, so no one will *know* if it's a boy or girl. I shall call your mother tonight, Amanda."

That night Mrs. Parris phoned Mrs. Fletcher who listened, then said: "Amanda already told me of the Christmas play. She's delighted she was chosen to play the part of Mary and more delighted that you want Christina to be the Infant Jesus."

"*Christina* — oh, how beautiful! And so appropriate," said Mrs. Parris.

Mrs. Fletcher sighed. "There is something we haven't told Amanda yet. We took Christina to the doctor last week…" Her voice broke slightly. "The doctor says Christina has no voice. She cannot cry, nor will she ever be able to speak."

Mrs. Parris was stunned. "I'm *so* sorry."

"I thought you should know. But if you still want Christina in the play, I shall bring her. With Amanda so near, I'm sure the baby won't be upset."

On the night of the play, little Christina lay in the manger, squirming and kicking her feet for all to see. She actually seemed to enjoy the attention.

At the climax of the play, the stage lights dimmed except for one spotlight focused on the manger. The figures of Joseph, Mary and the Wise Men knelt in prayer. Offstage, the chorus began to sing, "It Came Upon the Midnight Clear…" And as they sang, the baby's arms waved.

As the last notes of the old song died away, Aaron McCloskey, dressed as an angel wearing dark horn-rimmed glasses, came out on stage. A blue spotlight held him in its light. He spread his arms wide and in a loud, high-pitched voice recited flatly, "May the Holy Birth bring joy into the hearts of each and every one of us this Christmas!"

He was supposed to leave the stage at this point, but instead, all the thoughts that had long been buried inside the boy came rushing out. In a voice that was now filled with genuine emotion he added: "And may my parents and Amanda's parents be friends again!" He turned and ran from the stage.

There was a stunned silence in the auditorium. From the rear of the auditorium someone said "Amen," and the applause began. Then, as if in agreement, a small cry came from the manger and a tiny arm waved vigorously.

Mrs. Fletcher leaped to her feet and raced onto the stage. She picked up the wailing Christina and held her up for all to see. "Praise God," she shouted, "it's a miracle!"

Word spread quickly about the miracle, for no one had known about Christina's condition. The following Sunday, everyone in River Fork was in church. The Fletchers and McCloskeys shared the same pew and Amanda hoped Christina wouldn't disturb the service.

Reverend Adams stepped to the pulpit. "Friends, I'm not going to try to understand or explain what happened in the school auditorium last night. But we sure saw a couple of miracles happen." He stared directly at the McCloskeys and Fletchers.

"I want to propose that we do something to remind us all of this great wonder. I propose we change the name of our town from River Fork to — Miracle."

The shouts and applause were enough to convince everyone it was a good idea.

Once again a baby had reached into the hearts of people and left the priceless gift of love. And to this day it's said you'll never find a town where there's more love than in the town of Miracle.

The Scarlet Robe

 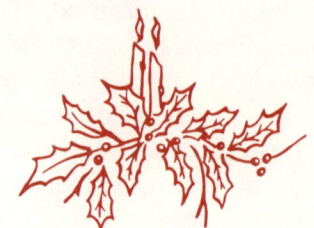

by Ann B. Benjamin

AARON was the richest sheep herdsman around Bethlehem. With his fine flock, excellent pastures and loyal shepherds, he was the happiest of men — except for one thing. He and Anna had only one child, their son David, who had been born with a twisted leg.

"He's the best pupil in the synagogue," Rabbi Ben Elim told Aaron and Anna. "But it's too bad — a boy should be able to run and play after his studies are finished."

Aaron thought on these things as he threaded his way through the crowded streets of Bethlehem. These thoughts always made his heart heavy — for though he was a rich man, only a miracle could make him rich in heart.

Aaron was on the street of the clothing peddlers, buying new cloaks for his shepherds, when he spied a scarlet robe among the merchandise of a Persian peddler. This was no ordinary robe — its cloth was of the finest silk and its color was a deep, rich red. It spoke of royalty. *Ah-h, this I must take to David...* he thought and quickly paid some gold coins for it.

When Aaron returned from the village, he told Anna and David of the crowds he had seen. "The village inn was full and overflowing," Aaron said excitedly, "and one man had brought his pregnant wife all the way from Nazareth...."

Though he was interested in all his father's excitement about the unusual events of the day, David was curious about the parcel his father was holding. When Aaron handed it to him he could scarcely untie it in his eagerness. The red silk robe glistened in the light.

"The robe is beautiful," little David cried, slipping it over his shoulders. "And warm too." He ran his fingers on the soft cloth.

"Why, it's fit for a king!" Anna exclaimed, adjusting the coat on David's small body. "And now you look like the son of a king!"

Just then two of Aaron's shepherd boys rushed into the house. "A new, bright star in the sky ...angels spoke to us." They spoke quickly, one after the other. "A baby was born in the innkeeper's stable last night...people flocked to see this extraordinary child." Aaron remembered what the Persian peddler had told him — there was a rumor all through the East that a new King was to be born. Surely *this* wasn't, it couldn't be....

"You *must* come and see for yourselves," the shepherds insisted. Running, carrying the crippled David, Aaron and Anna reached the stable cave which was lighted by a bright star from the heavens. There in the manger was the Baby. They wondered, *could this be the Messiah, the King? The Scriptures did say He would come from Bethlehem.*

David gazed at the tiny infant and at the Baby's parents who seemed so happy though poor. "His mother and father love him, don't they? But they have no clothes for him." He looked at his father.

"Do you think he is cold? Maybe...Father, may I give him my new robe? You said it was fit for a king."

Aaron looked at his son thoughtfully. "Go ahead, David. Do what you have to do," he said.

Slowly David took off his robe, crawled near the manger and spread his scarlet robe over the sleeping infant. The Baby stirred in His sleep. David turned to crawl back to his parents, then gasped. With a look of wonder and disbelief on his face he slowly stretched out his twisted leg, feeling no pain at all. He managed to get to his feet, stand at his full stature for a moment and then *walked* to his waiting parents.

Later they remembered the prophecy: "He comes to preach good news to the poor, to proclaim release to the captives, the recovering of sight to the blind, to heal the lame, to set at liberty those who are oppressed, and to proclaim the acceptable year of the Lord..." They knew that He indeed had come and they had met Him.

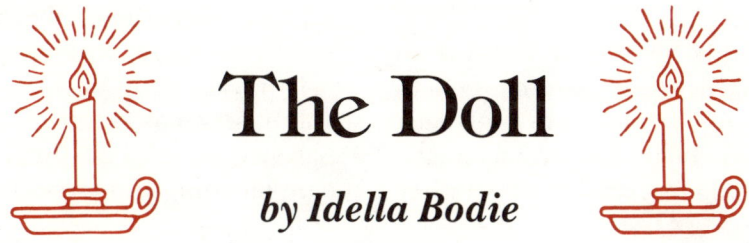

The Doll
by Idella Bodie

"MAMMA—" I pulled at my mother's skirt and pointed to the doll on the shelf of the department store. Mamma knew I had my heart set on a doll whose eyes would open and close.

It was 1933 and Christmas lay three weeks away. Mamma had taken us children on our annual trek from our quiet, rural home near Ridge Spring, South Carolina to the big, bustling city of Columbia to see the decorations and to tell Santa Claus we wanted black high-topped shoes and stockings for Christmas. It had been a hard year and money was scarce.

My father, a man of few words, had said "I doubt there'll be any toys in Santa's bag this year."

And Mamma had nodded in agreement, adding how lucky we were to live on a farm.

Careful to stay close to Mamma, I gazed in adoration at the doll. Her eyes were blue, and I could tell she would go to sleep when I laid her down. She had a rose bud of a mouth and a pale pink organdy dress and bonnet. I longed to hold her, but I was far too shy to ask.

In the following days — chilling winds sliced across our rolling farm, pushing us closer around the hickory fire. Cold gusts flickered the lamps as Daddy went in and out to do the chores; water froze in our wash basins. On long evenings I laid my head on our German shepherd and thought of the doll.

"Mamma," I'd try now and then. "I don't need any shoes. I want that doll." I could double the cardboard inside my shoe.

Always her answers were vague. Once I pressed her too far. "Oh," she said, "stop fretting. Santa may not make it at all this year."

When Christmas Eve finally came, I curled under the heaviness of the patchwork quilts, still yearning for the doll, and tried my best to lie still. As I asked God for the last time to let me have the doll, I remembered my Sunbeam leader, Miss Katie, and the stories she told us each Wednesday afternoon at the church. "If you prayed and believed," she said, "then your prayers would be answered." Still, I knew my prayers must end with "Thy will be done." Maybe God didn't want me to have the doll.

At dawn I awakened with a start. My heart quivered as I slipped from my covers to the iciness of the wooden floor.

At the parlor door my world reeled — *the doll leaned against a shoe box.*

Believing in my child's heart that this was all Santa's doing, I hurried to my parents' bed to show them my treasure. Then I took my doll back to bed with me. There I clutched her to my heart, her beautiful eyes closing in sleep until my father built the fire and we all got up to see our shoes.

From then on the cherished doll transformed my days. Her cloth body yielded to my love as I made her clothes, took her on walks in the sun-warmed pasture, let her soar in the great swing hanging from the oak, showed her new-born piglets and calves tottering on frail legs, and put her to bed at night. On special days I took her to the corn fields where I gave her silken hair from the golden tassels to go on her beautifully shaped head.

To this day I can shut my eyes and see her again under the tree that icy December morning. True, the doll was a material possession that I had coveted with a longing only a child can know. Yet through the years it has come to mean far more. I know now just how poor my parents were that year, how much sacrifice the doll meant. And today — over forty years later — I know that the miracle of Christmas belongs to those who give.

If my spirit for the Holy Season ever wanes, I gaze at that doll. Her face is cracked; the china blue eyes have faded; the fraying cloth of her body bears darning. Yet to me she is more beautiful then ever. Remembering, my heart prepares itself once more for the precious gift of the Spirit.

In recapturing and reliving my most memorable Christmas, I recall the immortality of my parents' love; love — given and received — the true meaning of Christmas.

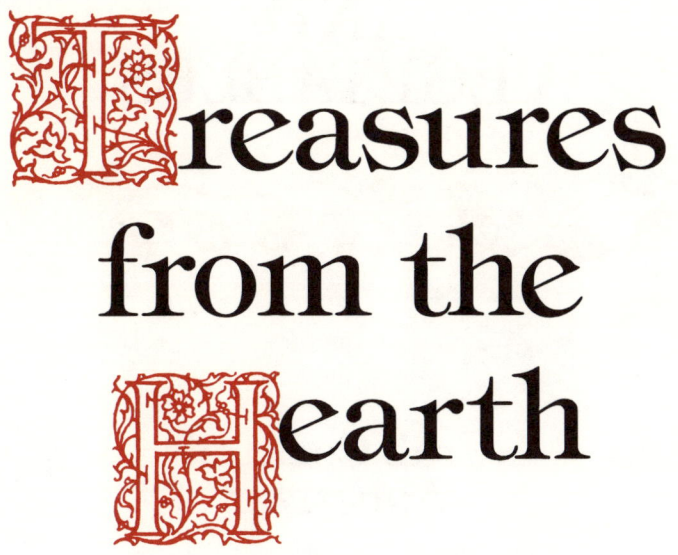

Treasures from the Hearth

A Festive Food Sampler

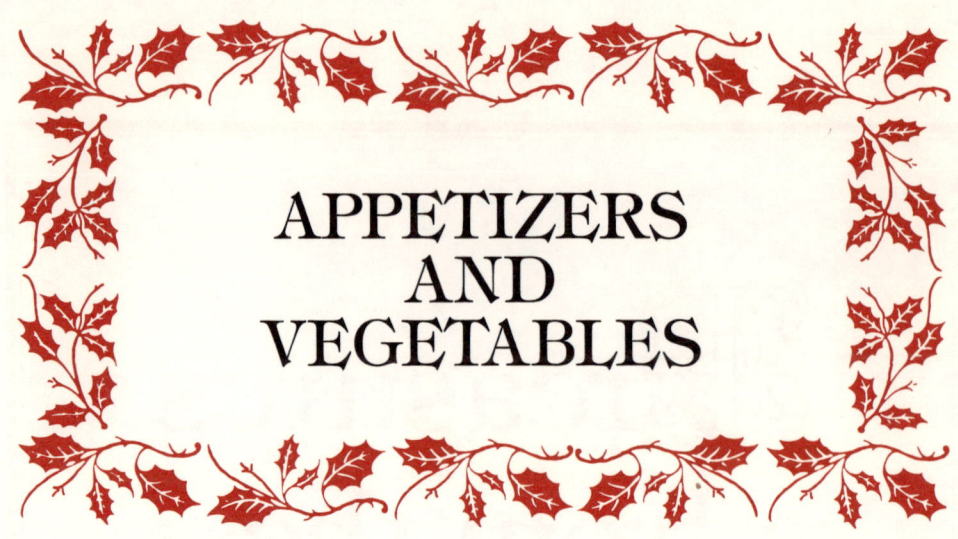

APPETIZERS AND VEGETABLES

Sour Cream Dip

1 pint sour cream
1 cup mayonnaise
2 Tbs. Dijon mustard
1 clove minced garlic
1 Tbs. minced onion
¼ cup parsley
salt to taste

—Terri Castillo

Crab Spread

1 8-oz. block of cream cheese, softened
1 can crabmeat
1 small jar cocktail sauce

Place drained crabmeat on top of cream cheese. Pour cocktail sauce over all. Spread crackers around the dish. Enjoy. —Terri Castillo

Crab Cocktail Appetizer

Line sherbet glasses with lettuce leaves. Add shredded crabmeat (canned) and finely chopped celery. Pour on the following sauce, using 2 tablespoonfuls to each portion:

1 cup catsup
½ cup chili sauce
2 Tbs. horseradish
2 Tbs. fresh lemon juice
salt and pepper to taste

—Terri Castillo

Sweet Potato Pie

1¼ cups (or 1 large can) mashed, cooked sweet potatoes
¼ cup brown sugar, liquid
¼ tsp. salt
¼ tsp. cinnamon
2 eggs
¾ cup milk
1 Tbs. butter, melted

Line an 8-inch pie plate with your favorite pastry. In a bowl, combine sweet potatoes with liquid brown sugar, salt and cinnamon. Beat together eggs, milk and melted butter and stir it into sweet potato mixture. Pour filling into the pastry shell and arrange walnut or pecan halves on top. Bake in a hot oven (400°F.) for 40-45 minutes.

— Christine Conti

Sweet Potato Casserole

4 Tbs. butter or margarine
¾ tsp. salt
⅓ cup orange juice
3 cups cooked, mashed sweet potatoes, hot
1 cup crushed pineapple, drained
8 marshmallows, cut in half

Add first four ingredients together, using 3 Tbs. butter or margarine; then add pineapple, folding into mixture. Put into 1-quart casserole, dot with remaining butter, top with marshmallow halves. Bake at 350°F. until marshmallows are puffed and brown. — Pat Sullivan

Hot Deviled Potatoes

1 package instant mashed potatoes
¼ cup dairy sour cream
½ tsp. prepared mustard
¼ tsp. sugar
1 Tbs. snipped green onion

Prepare 2 servings of potatoes according to package directions. Stir in remaining ingredients. Spoon into 2 foil baking shells. Sprinkle with paprika. Bake at 350°F. about 20 minutes, or till heated through. Serves 2. Double recipe for 4-5 people.

—Terri Castillo

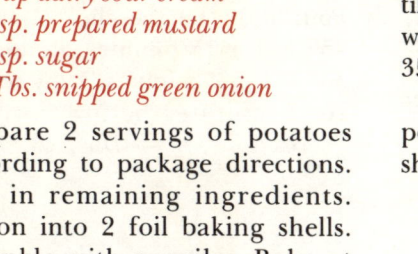

Sweet Potatoes in Orange Cups

8 large seedless oranges
2 cans sweet potatoes, drained
8 Tbs. melted butter
salt and pepper to taste

Cut off orange tops to a depth of 1½ inches. Scoop out all pulp. Strain and reserve ⅓ cup of the juice. Mash together the potatoes, butter, juice, salt, pepper, and heap into orange cups. Bake 350°F. for half hour. Garnish with orange-rind curls. — Phyllis Walk

Twice-Baked Potatoes

5 lbs. large baking potatoes
2 cups sour cream
1 cup half-and-half cream
1 cup chopped green onions
   and stems

Bake potatoes until done; cut in half and scrape out into mixing bowl. Use hand mixer and beat at low speed until mashed, then add all the other ingredients and beat till fluffy. Place in casserole and dot with butter. Bake 45 minutes at 350°F.

If you wish, you can mound the potato mixture in the hollowed shells, and bake. — Pat Sullivan

Candied Yams

3 lbs. yams
⅛ lb. butter
1 tsp. nutmeg
1 tsp. cinnamon
1 cup brown sugar
½ cup maple syrup
1 cup water

Peel yams and slice into halves or quarters. Place in pan with 2 cups of water. Cover and boil for 30 minutes or until yams are tender. Remove yams and place in pan or pyrex baking dish. Place slices of butter on yams. Sprinkle nutmeg and cinnamon and brown sugar over yams. Pour maple syrup over this. Add cup of water from water yams were boiled in. Pour into one corner of the dish. Place in 375°F. oven. Baste yams every 15 minutes. Bake until a deep orange or until a golden brown. About 2 hours.

— Oscar H. Greene

Maria's Broccoli-Rice Casserole

1½ cups raw rice, cooked
2 packages frozen, chopped
   broccoli, cooked
1 large onion, chopped
1 stick margarine
2 cans cream of chicken soup*
1 jar (16 oz.) soft American
   cheese

Sauté onion in margarine. Add soft American cheese and stir until melted. Add soup, rice and broccoli. Put into casserole dishes. Cover and bake at 350°F. for 1 hour. These casseroles may be frozen, baked or unbaked.

*If mixture seems dry, add 1 soup can of milk— Penny V. Schwab

Green Bean Casserole

2 cans french-style green beans,
   drain one can, keep juice
   from other can
1 can cream of mushroom soup
1 can french-fried onion rings

Mix beans with mushroom soup and juice from one can of the beans. Sprinkle the french-fried onion rings evenly over top after putting the mixture in a casserole dish. Bake 25 minutes at 275°F.

— Pat Sullivan

Yummy Peas

1 box frozen peas
½ cup lettuce, thinly sliced
3 green onions w/stems, sliced
2 Tbs. margarine

Cook peas, drain, add margarine. Toss in lettuce and green onions. Variation: add other cooked vegetables, like brussel sprouts.

—Terri Castillo

Dustin's Christmas Quiche

½ large onion
½ pound bacon (smoked)
1½ cups Swiss cheese
1 Tbs. flour
3 eggs
½ cup half-and-half
½ tsp. salt
dash nutmeg
dash cayenne

Cook already-prepared pie crust until done and still very light in color. Slice the onion and break into rings. Fry in margarine until tender. Drain, and place on bottom of crust. Fry the bacon until very crisp. Drain, and crumble over onion. Grate the cheese and toss it with the flour before sprinkling it on top of the bacon. Beat the eggs, add the cream and seasonings. Pour into the pie shell. Bake at 450°F. for 15 minutes. Reduce to 350°F. for 15 minutes. Allow to cool 10-15 minutes before cutting. Serves 4-6. — *Dee Ann Palmer*

SALADS

Cranana Salad

4 cups grated, raw cranberries
2 diced bananas
2 peeled and diced oranges
1 cup chopped walnuts
4 Tbs. honey

Toss the above thoroughly and serve in lettuce cups. Serves 6 to 8.
— *Phyllis Walk*

Flapper Salad

2 cups mandarin orange sections, drained
2 cups pineapple chunks, drained
2 cups white seedless grapes, halved
1 cup flaked coconut
½ cup maraschino cherries, halved and drained
2 cups miniature marshmallows
1 cup whipped cream
1 cup sour cream
2 Tbs. powdered sugar

Fold powdered sugar and sour cream into whipped cream. Mix in all the other ingredients, folding into mix evenly. Refrigerate overnight. Serve on a lettuce leaf.
— *Pat Sullivan*

Christmas Cranberry Salad

1 lb. cranberries, ground with 1 large orange, seeded but not peeled
2 packages red gelatin
2 cups boiling water
1 cup chopped pecans
1 15-oz. can crushed pineapple

Dissolve gelatin in boiling water. Add other ingredients and pour into large mold. Chill until set. Unmold on greens, and top individual servings with miniature cream cheese balls or fluffy mayonnaise.

FLUFFY MAYONNAISE

Whip ½ cup heavy cream until

stiff; fold in 1 cup of mayonnaise, blending well.

CREAM CHEESE BALLS

Using a melon-baller dipped in hot water, form cream cheese into small balls. Roll each in chopped nuts. Use to top salads.

— *Penny V. Schwab*

Mamie Tom's Christmas Salad

2 large oranges
2 bananas
2 red apples
8 1-oz. can crushed pineapple, drained
1½ cups miniature white marshmallows
  small bottle maraschino cherries
4 oz. diced pecans
2 oz. flaked coconut

A few minutes before serving, dice the fresh fruit into a bowl. Add drained pineapple and mix. Add nuts. Slice the cherries and mix them in. Add some of their juice to taste. Add the marshmallows and coconut last. Serves 8.

— *Dee Ann Palmer*

Christmas Wreath Salad

1 29-oz. can peach halves
1 29-oz. can pear halves
1 15¼-oz. can pineapple slices
1 16-oz. can whole, peeled apricots
1 17-oz. jar spiced crab apples
1 8-oz. package cream cheese, softened
  red maraschino cherries
1½ lbs. red and green grapes
2 slightly beaten egg whites
½ cup sugar
  curly endive

Drain canned fruits and chill. Dry chilled peaches and pears well on paper toweling. Fill hollows with half of the cream cheese. Put a cherry in the center of two halves of fruit before pressing together. Pipe remaining cream cheese through pastry tube to seal two halves.

To frost grapes: dip bunches of grapes into slightly beaten egg white. Drain off egg white; dip in sugar. Place on rack to dry for 1 to 2 hours.

Arrange bed of curly endive on large platter. Arrange fruit in circle. Small nut balls may add color to the ring by cutting an 8-oz. package of cream cheese into 8 pieces. Roll into balls, roll in crushed nuts, and tuck into ring.   — *Zona B. Davis*

Poinsettia Salad

1 No. 2½ can pear halves
½ cup red cinnamon drops
1 Tbs. vinegar
1 bunch watercress
4 tsp. grated sharp Cheddar cheese

Combine syrup from pears with cinnamon drops and vinegar and heat to boiling. Cut each pear half into 4 lengthwise slices to represent petals and simmer in syrup for 20 minutes, or until well colored. Chill. Arrange watercress on 4 salad plates. On each, arrange 8 petals clockwise, each curving toward the center to represent a flower. Sprinkle 1 teaspoon grated cheese in center of each flower.

— *Zona B. Davis*

Lime French Dressing

½ cup olive oil or salad oil
¼ cup lime juice
½ tsp. salt
  few grains cayenne
2 Tbs. sugar or honey
  drops of food coloring

— *Zona B. Davis*

BREAD AND BISCUITS

Zucchini Bread

*3 cups grated zucchini
   (or squash or pumpkin)*
3 eggs
2 cups sugar
1 cup oil
2 tsp. vanilla
3 cups flour
1 tsp. salt
1 tsp. baking powder
1 tsp. baking soda
1 tsp. cinnamon
1 cup chopped walnuts

Beat eggs and sugar; add grated zucchini and mix together. Add oil and vanilla, and stir. Stir in all other dry ingredients and, finally, add nuts; then pour into 2 greased and floured pans. Bake for 1 hour and 10 minutes at 350°F. or until a broomstraw or wisk inserted into the loaf comes out dry. Makes two loaves. Bread may be frozen for future use.   — *Naomi Lawrence*

Easy Fruit Bread

½ cup sugar
⅓ cup butter or margarine
½ tsp. salt
½ cup boiling water
¾ cup evaporated milk
2 eggs, beaten
¼ cup warm water
1 package yeast
1 cup mixed candied fruit
¼ tsp. lemon or vanilla flavoring
4½ cups sifted unbleached flour

Combine sugar, butter, salt and boiling water in large mixing bowl. Add evaporated milk. Dissolve yeast in warm water. Add to sugar mixture. Stir in eggs, candied fruit and flavoring. Add flour, 1 cup at a time, beating until fairly smooth after each addition. Cover, let rise in warm draft-free place for 1½ hours. Beat batter down. Turn into well-greased 10-inch tube pan and spread evenly. Let rise in warm place for 45 minutes. Bake in preheated 375°F. oven for 45-55 minutes or until tests down. Remove from pan immediately. Cool. While still slightly warm, ice immediately with confectioners sugar icing: ⅔ cup confectioners sugar mixed with 1½ Tbs. evaporated milk and ¼ tsp. vanilla. If desired, sprinkle chopped nuts on top, or decorate with pecan halves and candied cherries.   — *Anne Lorimer*

Mincemeat Swirlibuns

½ cup margarine
2 packages yeast
1 egg
4 cups unsifted flour
¾ cup milk
½ cup sugar
2 tsp. salt
1 lb., 12-oz. jar mincemeat

Scald milk; add sugar, salt, margarine. Cool to lukewarm. Dissolve yeast in ½ cup *warm* water. Add milk mixture, egg, 2 cups flour; beat until smooth. Stir in 2 cups flour. Cover tightly. Refrigerate at least 2 hours. Dough may be kept in refrigerator 3 days. Divide dough in half. On lightly floured board, roll each half to an 18 x 9-inch rectangle. Spread with mincemeat. Roll up each half from long side, as for jelly roll. Seal edges. Cut into

60

1½-inch slices; place, cut side up, in greased muffin cups. Cover. Let rise in warm place until doubled, about 1 hour. Bake at 350°F. for 20-25 minutes, or until done. When cool, frost with confectioners sugar frosting. Makes 24.
— *Anne Lorimer*

Think-Ahead Bran Muffins

In large bowl combine

- 1 15-oz. box (7 cups) raisin bran flakes
- 5 cups unsifted all-purpose flour
- 2 cups sugar
- 5 tsp. soda
- 2½ tsp. salt.

Mix well.

Then add:

- 4 cups milk blended with
- 2 Tbs. vinegar
- 1 cup vegetable oil
- ½ cup molasses
- 4 beaten eggs

Mix well again. Store covered in refrigerator and use as needed. When ready to bake, fill muffin pan cups ⅔ full. Bake in preheated 400°F. oven for 15 to 20 minutes. Batter will keep in refrigerator for 6 weeks.
— *Isabel Champ*

Holiday Ham and Sausage Biscuits

Bake biscuits by your grandmother's recipe, the biscuit-mix box, or fresh from the dairy case. Make twice as many as you think you need. (Leftovers can be frozen.)

While biscuits bake, cook small sausage patties to fit; trim ham slices to size. Drain sausage on paper towels.

Butter split biscuits while they're hot. Slide ham or sausage between layers. Serve at once, or allow to cool, cover with foil and refrigerate until party time. To reheat, allow 20 minutes at 350°F., remove foil cover, heat 5 minutes more.

Note: Look for tiny biscuit cutters for party biscuits, space one inch apart in pan for crusty goodness. Don't waste time making small biscuits for men, however.

Tip: Serve with hot coffee, party punch or tall pitchers of orange juice or cranberry cocktail.
— *Charlotte Fowler Allen*

Christmas Morning Sourdough Pancakes

- 2 cups flour
- 2 cups warm water
- 1 package dry yeast or 1 yeast cake

Mix well. Place in a warm place overnight. In the morning put ½ cup of the starter in a scalded pint jar with tight cover and store in cool place. Never use a metal container or leave a metal spoon in the starter.

Place the starter in a mixing bowl, add 2 cups warm water, 2 cups flour, beat well, and put it in a warm place to develop overnight.

In the morning the batter will double in size, covered with air bubbles, and have a pleasant, yeasty odor. After spooning ½ cup of the starter into the keeping jar, add to the remaining batter, beating with a fork to blend:

- 2 eggs
- 1 tsp. soda
- 1 tsp. salt
- 1 Tbs. sugar

Lastly, add 1 Tbs. melted fat. Then pour the batter onto a sizzling griddle, turning once. Serve them golden brown and slathered with homemade butter, ready for hot sugar syrup, molasses or honey.
— *Zona B. Davis*

MEAT AND DRESSINGS

Polynesian Ham

12 cups diced ham
8 Tbs. margarine
8 small green peppers, cut into strips
3 1 lb. cans pineapple tidbits
2 cups brown sugar
8 Tbs. cornstarch
2 cups vinegar
2 cups chicken stock or bouillon
8 tsp. soy sauce
1 16-oz. can mushroom pieces

Brown ham cubes lightly in margarine, add pepper strips and pineapple with syrup. Cover and simmer 15 minutes. Mix brown sugar, cornstarch and add to vinegar, chicken stock and soy sauce. Add ham mixture, mushrooms and liquid. Stir until thickened. Serves 25.
— *Janet Shaffer*

Turkey Olé

1 1½ lb. leftover turkey, boned
1 1 lb. can sliced tomatoes, drained, or 2 fresh tomatoes, sliced
1 4-oz. can diced green chiles, drained
1 4-oz. can sliced ripe olives, drained
2 cups sour cream
2 ripe avocados, peeled and sliced
2 cups cheddar and Jack cheese, grated

Line bottom of 13¾ x 8¾ x 1¾-inch baking dish with sliced tomatoes. Sprinkle chiles and olive on top, dot with sour cream. Add sliced avocados and cover evenly with turkey. Cover all ingredients evenly with cheeses. Bake in moderate oven (350°F.) 25-35 minutes, or until cheese is bubbly and entire dish is heated through. Allow to cool a few minutes.
— *Carolyn E. Phillips*

Chicken Molé Poblano

2 3-lb. broiler-fryers, cut into serving pieces
  water
1 onion
1 bay leaf
  salt
2 dried ancho chiles
4 dried mulato chiles
3 dried pasilla chiles
3 Tbs. vegetable oil
1 small onion, chopped
2 garlic cloves, peeled
3 small tomatoes, peeled, seeded and chopped
  vegetable oil
½ cup bread crumbs
1 tortilla, toasted and crumbled
½ cup almonds
3 Tbs. pepitas
½ cup peanuts
2 Tbs. sesame seeds
2 Tbs. white raisins
½ tsp. anise seeds
2 whole cloves
3 peppercorns
½ tsp. cinnamon
2 oz. semi-sweet chocolate

4 tsp. sugar
4 cups chicken broth
 salt
 freshly ground pepper

Place chicken pieces in large pot. Add water to cover, sliced onion, bay leaf and salt to taste. Bring to boil and cook, covered, for 1 hour. Drain, reserving stock. Rinse chiles. Heat 3 tablespoons oil in skillet. Fry chiles 5 minutes, taking care not to burn. Drain on towel and place in blender with 1 cup of water until pureed. Take out of blender. Set aside.

Place chopped onion, garlic and tomatoes in blender and mix until smooth. Heat 1 tablespoon of oil in skillet. Stir bread crumbs, tortilla, almonds, peanuts and pepitas until browned but not burned. Add the bread and nuts mixture, with sesame seeds, anise seeds, raisins, cloves, peppercorns and cinnamon to onion mixture in blender. Process until pureed, adding about 2 tablespoons of chicken stock as needed.

Heat 2 tablespoons of oil in flameproof casserole. Add pureed onion mixture. Stir for 10 minutes over medium heat. Add chile puree. Cook, stirring constantly, for 5 minutes, gradually adding 4 cups of broth from chicken stock. Stir in chocolate and sugar until dissolved. Add salt to taste. Add chicken pieces to casserole. Cover and cook over very low heat for 1 hour, taking care not to burn. Sauce should be dark and have the consistency of heavy cream. If necessary, thin with some chicken stock.

Place a piece of chicken on each plate, cover with sauce and sprinkle with sesame seeds just before serving. This dish is usually served with black beans and rice and a green or avocado salad. Serves 6 to 8.

— *Pat Ayres*

Hamburger Hotcakes

3 egg yolks (save whites)
½ lb. hamburger
¼ tsp. baking powder
½ tsp. salt
 dash pepper
1 tsp. lemon juice
1 Tbs. minced parsley
3 egg whites, beaten stiff

Mix all ingredients except egg whites. When thoroughly mixed, fold in egg whites. Drop by spoonfuls on hot, greased griddle. When puffed and brown, turn and brown other side. Serves 4.— *Isabel Champ*

Hamburger Stew

1 lb. hamburger
1 diced onion

Brown lightly in a heavy kettle.

Add:

 1 cup diced potatoes
 1 cup sliced carrots
 ½ cup diced celery
 ½ cup uncooked rice
 ½ tsp. pepper
 1 No. 2 can or 1 quart canned tomatoes
 1 Tbs. salt
1½ quarts water

Combine all ingredients and simmer at least 1 hour.

— *Isabel Champ*

A Merry Meat Pie

1 pie crust
1 medium chopped onion
1½ lbs. ground pork
1 tsp. salt
1 tsp. poultry seasoning
⅔ cup water
 dash pepper

Cook all ingredients except pie crust in pot on top of stove until the meat turns gray. Drain, cool, and then turn into pie crust. Bake for 1 hour at 350°F.

— *Marilyn M. Angers*

Family-Style Roast Chicken and Dressing

12 cups dry or stale bread crumbs
 2 cups finely chopped onion
 4 cups finely diced celery
 1 lb. bulk pork sausage
 3 tsp. salt
 2 tsp. sage
 1 cup broken walnut meats
 ½ tsp. black pepper
 2 cups cold water
 2 frying chickens, quartered

Sauté sausage, onions and celery in frying pan until vegetables are barely tender, then add salt, pepper, sage and walnuts, and cook a minute longer. In the meantime, sprinkle the water over the bread crumbs, evenly. Add the cooked ingredients to the bread mixture and blend well. Place in open roast pan and put quartered frying chickens on top, one piece per person. Cover with foil and bake at 350°F. for about 1 hour; then remove foil and bake until done and chicken is brown and crispy.

— *Pat Sullivan*

Sausage Stuffing

1 or 2 loaves dry bread, cubed
1 to 1½ lbs. bulk sausage
1 onion, chopped fine
1 tsp. sage
salt and pepper to taste
1 egg
1 cup boiling water

Mix all ingredients and blend with 2 knives or pastry tool as you would pie crust. Fill turkey cavity and truss. Put remaining dressing in casserole and bake, covered, along with turkey the last 40 minutes. Remove cover and let brown another 10 minutes if desired.

— *Phyllis Walk*

Southern Dressing, Texas Style

For 16-pound turkey

4 quarts crumbs consisting of:
   1¼ quarts cornbread crumbs
   1¼ quarts homemade biscuit crumbs
   1½ quarts white breadcrumbs
1⅓ cups margarine
3 cups chopped celery
¾ cup chopped parsley
½ cup chopped onion
2 tsp. sage
2 tsp. salt

Place crumbs in large bowl. Melt margarine in frying pan. Add celery, parsley and onion. Cook a few minutes until soft. Add seasonings. Add to crumbs and mix thoroughly. — *Dee Ann Palmer*

Best-Ever Turkey Dressing

2 loaves white bread, a few days old; break into small pieces
1 stalk celery, chopped
2 large onions, chopped
1 lb. bulk pork sausage meat
1 cup broken walnut meats
2 tsp. ground sage
1 tsp. black pepper
1 tsp. salt
½ stick butter

Put bread pieces in large colander and run under water. Then squeeze most of water out. Put in large bowl. Meantime, sauté pork sausage meat till brown, breaking up large pieces with spoon. Add celery, onions and nuts, and cook at low heat for 5 minutes. Add all the seasonings and butter, and cook 1 minute longer. Add this to bread when cooled to lukewarm, and blend well. — *Patricia Sullivan*

Busy Bee Raisin Dressing

1 loaf dry bread or lightly toasted bread

Break up into a mixing bowl. Measure 1 cup raisins; add enough water to moisten well and let set. Use 2 or more cups of chicken or beef broth so as to moisten bread well. Add:

2 beaten eggs
½ cup diced celery
¼ cup diced apples
¼ cup diced onions
1 cup sugar
Salt and pepper to taste

Mix well; add raisins, stirring in well. Turn into buttered baking pan or casserole (bake with lid on). Put dabs of butter on top of dressing before covering. Bake at 375°F. for 30 minutes or until done.

—*Zona B. Davis*

Turkey Stuffing

2 loaves white bread
1 lb. (4 quarter-pound sticks) margarine or butter
1 cup chopped celery
1 cup chopped walnuts
salt, pepper, poultry seasoning, onion powder

Crumble sliced or unsliced bread into small chunks. Melt margarine or butter in large skillet or pot and stir in bread crumbs. Keep flame low. Stir crumbs until they've all absorbed margarine or butter and are slightly browned. Remove from heat and stir in remaining ingredients. STUFF! into 10 to 12 lb. bird. — *Naomi Lawrence*

DESSERTS

Pumpkin Brownies

- ¼ cup flour
- ¼ cup instant potatoes
- 1 tsp. baking powder
- ½ tsp. salt
- 1½ tsp. cinnamon
- ¼ tsp. allspice
- ¼ tsp. ginger
- ½ cup margarine
- ¼ cup sugar
- 1 egg
- ¾ cup canned pumpkin
- ¼ cup chopped pecans

Sift together flour, baking powder, salt, spices. Then mix in instant potatoes.

Melt margarine, stir in sugar, egg, pumpkin. Add to sifted ingredients and nuts. Stir till well blended, bake in well-oiled square pan for 40 minutes at 350°F. Cool pan on wire rack. Turn out, cut in squares. Frost or eat plain or serve with topping or ice cream.

— *Phyllis Walk*

Praline Cheesecake

CRUST
- 1 cup graham cracker crumbs
- 3 Tbs. sugar
- 3 Tbs. butter, melted

CAKE MIXTURE
- 3 8-oz. packages cream cheese, softened
- ¼ cup firmly packed brown sugar
- 3 eggs
- 2 Tbs. flour
- ½ cup chopped pecans
- 1½ tsp. vanilla

In a bowl combine ingredients for crust. With the back of a large spoon press the mixture into the bottom of an 8-inch springform pan. Bake the crust for 10 minutes in 350°F. oven.

In a bowl beat cream cheese. Soften with brown sugar until mixture is fluffy. Beat in eggs, one at a time, and sift in flour. Add chopped pecans and vanilla. Pour mixture into the springform pan. Bake 350°F. for 55 minutes. Let cake cool in pan. Chill at least 3 hours. (Cake can be frozen.)

— *Nancy C. Galya*

The World's Best Brownies

- 2 sticks margarine
- 2 squares unsweetened chocolate
- 2 cups sugar
- 3 eggs
- 1 cup flour
- ½ tsp. salt
- 1 tsp. vanilla
- 1 cup walnuts
- greased and floured 9 x 13-inch pan

Melt margarine, chocolate and sugar in top of double boiler — cool slightly. Add eggs, vanilla, flour, salt and nuts. Pour into prepared pan. Bake at 350°F. for 25 minutes.

Sprinkle with powdered sugar while warm. Cut into 1-inch squares for cookie plate, or larger squares to serve a la mode.

— *Betty R. Schneider*

Rumford Doughnuts

4 cups flour
⅔ tsp. salt
3 tsp. baking powder
¾ cup sugar
1 tsp. grated nutmeg
1 egg
2 Tbs. melted shortening
1 cup milk, approximately
powdered sugar

Sift the dry ingredients together. Beat egg until light and use with the melted shortening and milk to form a light dough. Turn onto floured board, roll half an inch thick, cut with a doughnut cutter and drop gently into the hot fat. As soon as the doughnuts rise to the top of the pan, turn them over, turning again 2 or 3 times during the cooking, which takes about 3 minutes. Drain on crumpled, soft paper and dust with powdered sugar.
— Janet Shaffer

Grandma's Chocolate Cake

1 cup (2 sticks) margarine
1 cup water
6 Tbs. cocoa

Put ingredients into saucepan and bring to a boil. Set aside.

½ cup buttermilk
1 tsp. soda
½ tsp. salt
1 tsp. vanilla
2 eggs
2 cups flour
2 cups sugar

Sift dry ingredients into bowl, then add eggs, vanilla and buttermilk. Beat well, and add hot cocoa mixture. Beat well again. Pour batter into 3 8-inch or 2 9-inch greased and floured cake pans or into 12 x 16-inch baking pan. Bake at 375°F. about 30 minutes

CREAM FILLING

1 cup cream
¾ cup sugar
6 Tbs. flour
2 egg yolks
½ tsp. vanilla

Combine ingredients, except vanilla. Cook in top of double boiler, stirring constantly until thick. Add vanilla. Spread generously between cake layers.

CHOCOLATE FROSTING

1 box (1 lb.) powdered sugar
1 stick margarine (softened)
4 Tbs. cocoa
½ cup chopped nuts
6 Tbs. milk — enough to make frosting of a spreading consistency

Combine all ingredients and beat well.

(Mixing ¼ cup of this frosting with the cream filling before spreading it between layers makes the cake especially good and moist.)
— Isabel Champ

Peanut Cake

Preheat the oven at 350°F.

⅔ cup butter
1 cup sugar
3 eggs
2¼ cups all-purpose flour
2 tsp. baking powder
⅔ cup milk
1 tsp. vanilla
1 Tbs. light corn syrup

Cream butter and sugar. Add eggs, one at a time. Sift all-purpose flour with baking powder and add alternately with milk. Add vanilla and light corn syrup. Bake in 4 9-inch greased cake pans. This will make thin layers.

ICING

1½ cups sugar
7½ Tbs. cold water
½ tsp. cream of tartar (rounded)
¼ tsp. salt
3 egg whites
1 tsp. vanilla

Mix sugar, cold water, cream of tartar and salt. Bring to a full boil on medium heat. Pour syrup slowly over unbeaten egg whites while beating at high speed with mixer. Add vanilla and beat until spreading consistency.

Ice one layer at a time and cover each layer with a thick sprinkling of peanuts.
— Sara Thomas

Forgotten Cake

5 egg whites
pinch of salt
½ tsp. cream of tartar
1½ cups sugar

Combine egg whites and salt; add cream of tartar, and beat until stiff. Add sugar gradually. Pour into 8 x 10-1 inch greased pan. Have oven preheated to 450°F. Put meringue in oven and let stand overnight. Turn oven off immediately after meringue is put in oven. DO NOT OPEN OVEN DOOR UNTIL MORNING (about 12 hours). Cover with whipped cream and let stand in refrigerator 4 hours. Top with strawberries, or use fresh strawberries with candy mint leaves for a festive appearance.
— Zona B. Davis

Sugarplum Cake

- ¾ cup butter (1½ sticks)
- 1¾ cups sugar
- 4 eggs
- 4 cups flour
- ¾ lb. candied orange slices, cut in pieces
- 1½ cups chopped pecans
- 1 package dates (½ lb., chopped)
- 1 can flaked coconut (3½ oz.)
- 1 tsp. baking soda
- 1 cup buttermilk
- 1 Tbs. lemon juice
- 2 tsp. grated orange rind

GLAZE

- 2 cups powdered sugar
- 1 cup orange juice
- 2 tsp. grated orange rind

Cream butter and sugar until fluffy; beat in eggs one at a time; sift half the flour over the orange slice bits, pecans, dates and coconut, tossing together. Sift remaining flour with baking soda and add alternately with buttermilk to creamed mixture.

Stir in flavorings. Mix in the dredged candy and fruit with your hands. Fill greased and floured tube pan or two 9 x 5-inch loaf pans. Bake in a pre-heated slow oven (300°F.) for about 1½ hours. Test to see if done after 1 hour and 15 minutes. If pan is large, it may take an extra 15 minutes. Remove cake from oven and let rest a few minutes before pricking with a skewer. Combine glaze ingredients and spoon over hot surface of the cake.
— Zona B. Davis

Irish Coffee Cake

Beat:

- 1 cup sugar
- ½ cup butter
- 2 eggs

Add:

- 1 cup sour cream or buttermilk

Sift together:

- 2 cups sifted flour
- ½ tsp. salt
- 1 Tbs. baking powder
- ½ tsp. vanilla

Combine, pour into 9 x 13-inch cake pan.

TOPPING (spread on coffee cake before baking)

- ⅓ cup brown sugar
- ¼ cup white sugar
- 1 Tbs. cinnamon
- ½ cup nutmeats

Bake at 350°F. for about 40 minutes.
— Frances Fowler Allen

Chocolate Yule Log

Beat until stiff (holds a point):

- ½ tsp. cream of tartar
- 6 egg whites

Beat in gradually until glossy:

- ½ cup sugar

Set aside.

Beat separately until thick and lemon-colored:

- 6 egg yolks

Beat in:

- ½ cup sugar

Sift together and beat into yolks:

- 4 Tbs. sifted flour
- 4 Tbs. cocoa
- ½ tsp. salt
- 1 tsp. vanilla

Carefully fold into egg-white mixture. Spread into 15½ x 10½-inch pan that has been lined with wax paper and greased with vegetable shortening. Bake in 350°F. oven until surface springs back when lightly touched with finger (20-25 minutes). Immediately turn onto a towel sprinkled with confectioners sugar, remove paper from cake and trim the sides slightly. Roll up completely from the long side and cool. Then spread a piece of waxed paper on the table, sprinkle again with confectioners sugar, and remove towel. Roll cake in waxed paper until ready to fill with whipped cream mixture. Cake roll must be cool when that is to be done.

WHIPPED CREAM MIXTURE

Beat until stiff:

- 1 pint heavy cream beaten with confectioner's sugar to taste. Could be from 2 to 5 Tbs.

When you have filled the log, frost with creamy chocolate icing and decorate with knife to look like a log. You may put green mint leaves and small candied cherries on top to represent holly. This may be frozen ahead of time, and brought out 2 hours before serving.

CHOCOLATE ICING

Mix ¾ cup sugar and ¾ cup cream or milk and cook over low heat just until it boils. Pour slowly over 1½ cups shaved chocolate (3 squares unsweetened and 4 ounces, or squares, German sweet chocolate). Beat until chocolate is melted and mixture is smooth. You may add more liquid if too thick. Spread on Yule Log and decorate.
— Ruth G. Roth

Loving Kindness Christmas Cupcakes

1 stick (½ cup) margarine
1 tsp. vanilla
1½ cups packed brown sugar
3 eggs
2¼ cups sifted flour
2 tsp. baking powder
1 tsp. baking soda
½ tsp. salt
1¼ cups mashed ripe bananas (3-4)
¼ cup milk
½ cup chopped nuts

Cream butter, vanilla and sugar until light and fluffy. Beat in eggs. Sift in flour, baking powder, soda and salt. Then add bananas and milk, mixing alternately with dry ingredients. Stir in walnuts. Fill muffin or biscuit tins with colorful cupcake papers and fill ⅔ full with batter. Bake at 350°F. about 15 minutes — or until top springs back when touched. Cool. Then, if desired, frost.
— Isabel Champ

Cream Cheese Frosting

2 packages cream cheese (3-oz. size)
3 cups unsifted powdered sugar
1 tsp. vanilla

Mix softened cream cheese until smooth. Gradually beat in powdered sugar and vanilla, and beat until smooth. Several drops of red or green food coloring could be added.
— Isabel Champ

Old-Fashioned Dried Fruitcake

1 cup dried apples
1 cup prunes
1 cup molasses
½ cup water
½ cup shortening
1 cup sugar
2 cups currants
¾ cup seeded raisins
¼ tsp. baking soda
2 cups flour
¼ tsp. salt
2 tsp. baking powder
2 tsp. mixed, ground spices

Simmer together slowly the apple, prunes, molasses and water, then cool. Cream shortening and sugar; add the currants, raisins and cooked fruit into which the soda (dissolved in 2 tsp. water) has been stirred. Then add the flour, salt, baking powder and spices. Mix thoroughly, turn into cake pan and bake in a slow — 300°F. oven about 1 hour. This cake should be kept at least a month before eating.
— Janet Shaffer

Bakeless Fruit Cake

½ lb. graham crackers
½ lb. dry, crisp cookies
½ lb. marshmallows, cut up
½ lb. dates, chopped
½ cup chopped walnuts
½ cup chopped pecans
½ cup thin cream
½ cup white corn syrup
1 cup favorite preserves or jam

Crush crackers and cookies fine; mix with other ingredients and press into pan lined with waxed paper. Let stand over night or longer. Top with whipped cream garnished with maraschino cherry.
— Zona B. Davis

Holiday Applesauce Cake

1 cup shortening
1 cup brown sugar
½ cup granulated sugar
1½ tsp. salt
3 eggs
2 cups applesauce
2 tsp. soda
1 tsp. each of cinnamon, cloves and nutmeg
2 cups of flour, sifted together

Mix together in the order given and fold in:

1 cup raisins
1 cup chopped dates
1 cup nuts and maraschino cherries mixed with 1 cup flour

Bake in a tube cake pan at 350°F. for 45 minutes to 1 hour.

CREAMY BUTTER FROSTING

½ cup (1 stick) butter
1 lb. package confectioners sugar
1 tsp. vanilla
⅛ tsp. salt
1 Tbs. milk or cream
1 egg

Cream butter until smooth. Add ⅓ of the sugar, and cream thoroughly. Add salt, milk and vanilla. Blend. Add unbeaten egg, and beat until smooth. Add remaining sugar. Beat until smooth. If frosting is a little thick, more milk or cream may be added.
— Zona B. Davis

Champ's Applesauce Cake

1 cup brown sugar
1 cup white sugar
2 cups applesauce
1 cup margarine

1 tsp. allspice
1 tsp. cinnamon
1 tsp. cloves
2 tsp. baking powder
2 tsp. soda
3 cups flour
1 cup raisins
1 (1 lb.) carton candied
   fruit (optional)
1 cup chopped nuts

Mix all ingredients together, reserving a little flour in order to flour candied fruits and raisins to keep them from sticking together. This is a large cake — will fill 4 greased and floured bread pans or one baking pan 10 x 16 inches (or one even a bit larger). Bake at 350°F. about 45 minutes. Needs no frosting.
— *Isabel Champ*

Holiday Mince Pie

1½ cups lean hamburger
1 cup water
1 tsp. salt

Simmer meat until done.

Add:

3 cups chopped apples
1 cup raisins
2 oranges, peeled and chopped
1 lemon, peeled and chopped,
   or 1 tsp. lemon juice
½ cup sugar
¼ cup white corn syrup
1 tsp. cinnamon
½ tsp. cloves
½ tsp. allspice

Cook 40 minutes. Fill unbaked pie shell; top with crust. Bake in 350°F. oven until crust is brown.
— *Zona B. Davis*

Candy's Honey Pumpkin Pie

(9-inch size)

2 eggs
1½ cups pumpkin
¾ cup evaporated milk
¾ cup honey
¼ cup orange juice
¼ tsp. grated orange rind
½ tsp. salt
¼ tsp. ginger
1 tsp. cinnamon
¼ tsp. cloves
1 Tbs. boiling water

Beat eggs, stir in next 6 ingredients. Measure spices into a cup, add boiling water and stir to make a smooth paste. Stir into pumpkin mixture. Pour into uncooked pastry shell. Preheat over to 425°F. Have rack 4 or 5 inches from bottom of oven, bake 15 minutes at 425°F. Lower temperature in oven to 325°F. and bake 25 minutes longer, or until toothpick inserted in center comes out clean.
— *Hope B. Friedman*

Candy's Pie Crust

(for double 10-inch pie)

3 cups whole wheat pastry flour
1½ cups shortening
1 tsp. salt
1 Tbs. vinegar
3 Tbs. water
1 large egg

Combine flour, salt, shortening, with pastry blender. Beat water, vinegar, and egg with fork and add to flour mixture. Chill one hour before rolling.— *Hope B. Friedman*

Whipped Lemon Pie

1 can evaporated milk
   (refrigerated for 24 hours)
1 small package lemon gelatin
½ cup sugar
1 cup boiling water
   juice and rind shavings of
   2 lemons

Mix gelatin, sugar, hot water and lemon juice and rind and jell slightly in refrigerator. Whip gelatin mix. Beat evaporated milk. Mix the two together and pour into graham-cracker crust (or your favorite pie crust.) Refrigerate. Makes 2 pies.
— *Terri Castillo*

Ann's Oklahoma Pecan Pie

1 unbaked 9-inch pie shell
3 eggs
⅔ cup sugar
½ tsp. salt
⅓ cup butter, melted
½ cup dark corn syrup
½ light corn syrup
1 cup Oklahoma paper-shell
   pecans

With rotary beater, mix all ingredients except pecans. Stir in pecans and pour into pie shell. Bake at 375°F. for 40-50 minutes. Pie is done when it is set 1 inch from edge of pie shell, but still soft in the center.
— *Penny V. Schwab*

That Pie

1 cup evaporated milk
3 eggs, separated
½ cup sugar
   pinch salt
½ tsp. nutmeg
1 Tbs. unflavored gelatin
¼ cup cold water
3 Tbs. rum flavoring
1 cup heavy cream, whipped
1 9-inch pie shell, baked
1 square grated bitter chocolate

Scald milk. Beat egg yolks with sugar, salt and nutmeg. Add milk slowly, continuing to beat. Return mixture to double boiler and cook until thickened. Soften gelatin in water and add to egg mixture. Chill until partially set. Fold in egg whites. Pour into pie shell and chill until firm. To serve, spread with whipped cream and sprinkle the grated chocolate over the top.
— Penny V. Schwab

Cranberry Mousse with Raspberry Sauce

3 cups fresh or fresh-frozen
   cranberries
1 cup sugar
1 quart cranberry-juice cocktail
3 envelopes unflavored gelatin
2 cups heavy cream, whipped

In a medium saucepan combine cranberries, sugar and 1 cup cranberry-juice cocktail. Heat to boiling, reduce heat and simmer 5 minutes uncovered. Stir gelatin into 1 cup cranberry juice to soften. Stir gelatin mixture into hot cranberry mixture. Add remaining cranberry juice and refrigerate until slightly thickened. Fold whipped cream into slightly thickened gelatin mixture and then pour into 2 quart mold. Chill until firm.
— Phyllis Walk

Raspberry Sauce

1 package frozen raspberries,
   thawed
1 jar (12. oz.) raspberry preserves

Press raspberries and juice through sieve. Discard seeds. Stir in preserves. Mix well and refrigerate. When ready to serve, loosen with knife and dip mold in warm water for a few seconds. Invert mold on plate. Garnish as desired with canned pears or mandarin oranges and serve each portion with sauce.
— Phyllis Walk

Quaker Plum Pudding

1 cup milk
3 cups bread crumbs
½ cup shortening, melted
1½ cups molasses
1 cup flour
1 tsp. soda
1 tsp. salt
2 tsp. cinnamon
¼ tsp. allspice
¼ tsp. cloves
½ cup raisins
½ cup citron

Pour the milk over crumbs. Blend in shortening and molasses. Sift together flour, soda, salt, cinnamon, allspice and cloves. Stir into bread mixture. Add raisins and citron. Pour into greased mold and steam 3 hours, having mold not more than ⅔ full. Cover and place on trivet in boiling water that comes halfway up around mold. Keep water at boiling point, adding boiling water as needed. Serve with sauce:

½ cup butter
1½ cups confectioners sugar
2 egg whites
½ tsp. vanilla

Blend confectioners sugar and butter. Beat in egg whites and add vanilla.
— Virginia Westervelt

Holiday Punch

5 quarts cranberry juice
5 cups sugar
4 cans pineapple juice (46 oz.)
5 Tbs. almond extract
10 quarts ginger ale

Combine all ingredients, add ginger ale when ready to serve. Make ice ring with cherries and thinly sliced lemon. To make the ice ring, fill ring mold with water, add thin slices of lemon and maraschino cherries, and freeze. When partially frozen, push lemon slices and cherries to bottom of mold and freeze solid. Serves 75.
— Janet Shaffer

Cranberry Cider

1 quart cider
1 quart cranberry juice
⅓ cup brown sugar
6 cloves
1 cinnamon stick
4 whole allspice

Heat, stir. Makes 8 mug-size servings.
—Terri Castillo

COOKIES

Spritz Cookies

1 lb. butter
1 cup sugar
2 eggs
4 cups flour
1 tsp. vanilla

Mix in the above order. Push through a cookie press or drop by teaspoonfuls on a cookie sheet. Bake at 400°F. for 8 to 10 minutes.
— *Peggy Brooke*

Peanut Butter Cookies

1 lb. margarine
1 lb. peanut butter (2 cups)
1 lb. sugar (2 cups)
1 lb. brown sugar
    (2 cups, packed)
4 eggs
1 Tbs. vanilla
1 Tbs. baking soda
2 tsp. salt
5 cups all-purpose flour

Mix ingredients in order given. Using a tablespoon, place cookies on a greased baking sheet. Bake 10 to 12 minutes at 350°F. Makes 100 cookies.
— *Janet Shaffer*

Oatmeal-Nut Cookies

1 cup sugar
1 cup raisins
1 tsp. cinnamon
2 cups oatmeal
1 cup nuts
1 tsp. baking powder
2 cups flour
¼ cup vegetable oil
2 eggs
4 Tbs. sweet milk
1 tsp. vanilla

Mix sugar and vegetable oil. Stir in slightly beaten eggs, milk and oatmeal. While stirring, sift in flour, with baking powder and cinnamon added. Drop spoonfuls of the mixture onto a greased cookie pan. Bake at 350°F., 8 to 10 minutes.
— *Marjorie Lindsey Brewer*

Jean's Chocolate Crackles

¼ cup vegetable oil
4 squares unsweetened chocolate, melted
2 cups sugar
4 eggs

2 tsp. vanilla
2 cups flour
2 tsp. baking powder
½ tsp. salt
confectioners sugar

Mix oil, chocolate and granulated sugar. Add eggs one at a time, blending well. Add vanilla, stir in flour, baking powder and salt. Chill several hours or overnight. Drop teaspoons of dough into confectioners sugar. Roll in confectioners sugar, shaping dough into ball. Place about 2 inches apart on a greased baking sheet. Bake at 350°F. for 10-12 minutes. Don't overbake.
— *Penny V. Schwab*

Currant-Almond Cookies

2 tsp. unsalted butter, softened and
1 lb. unsalted butter, softened
2 cups sugar
4 eggs
2 cups flour
1 tsp. vanilla
½ cup finely chopped, blanched almonds
¼ cup currants

71

Preheat oven to 375°F. With a pastry brush or paper towel, spread a 12 x 18-inch jellyroll pan with 2 teaspoons of butter. Cream the pound of butter and sugar together until light and fluffy. Beat in the eggs, 1 at a time. Beat in flour and vanilla. Spread batter evenly onto the pan. Sprinkle the surface with almonds and currants, and bake 20-25 minutes, until the surface is light gold. Remove from oven and let cool in pan. With a sharp knife, cut into small triangles or squares.

Can be made two weeks in advance, but then the cookies must be wrapped in aluminum foil or placed in airtight tin and stored in cool place. Makes about 2 dozen small cookies. — *Virginia Westervelt*

Mother's Holiday Hermits

 1 *cup butter*
1½ *cups brown sugar*
 3 *eggs*
 1 *cup chopped raisins*
 1 *tsp. soda dissolved in 2 Tbs. milk*
    nutmeg, cinnamon and cloves to taste

Roll out on board, cut in squares and bake at 350°F. for 10-12 minutes. — *Janet Shaffer*

Bustle Oven Gingerbread Cookies

1 *cup sugar*
1 *cup molasses*
1 *cup lard*
1 *cup hot water*
2 *eggs*

Combine; rinse molasses out of cup with the hot water. Add eggs. Mix together with the following:

1 *tsp. soda*
1 *heaping tsp. ginger*
1 *tsp. cinnamon*
½ *tsp. salt*
6 *or 7 cups flour, (use ⅓ whole wheat)*

Roll out on floured board and cut with cookie cutter. Bake at 350°F. 10-15 minutes. — *Zona B. Davis*

Quick Ginger Cookies

Cream together:

1 *cup sugar*
¾ *cup butter*

Then add:

1 *beaten egg*
2 *Tbs. molasses*
2 *tsp. baking soda*
1 *tsp. ginger*
1 *tsp. cinnamon*
2 *cups flour*

Mix using an electric mixer. Roll dough into round balls the size of walnuts. Place them on an ungreased cookie sheet. DO NOT flatten out the dough. Bake for 8 to 10 minutes in a 375°F. oven and remove. — *Oscar H. Greene*

Butterscotch Cookies with Burnt-Butter Icing

 ½ *cup butter*
1½ *cups brown sugar*
 2 *eggs*
2½ *cups flour*
 ½ *tsp. baking powder*
 1 *tsp. soda*
 ½ *tsp. salt*
 1 *cup sour cream*
 1 *tsp. vanilla*
 ⅔ *cup walnuts*

Cream butter, add sugar gradually, and cream thoroughly. Blend in well-beaten eggs. Sift flour before measuring. Sift flour, baking powder, soda and salt together, and add to creamed mixture alternately with sour cream. Blend in vanilla and nuts. Chill until dough is firm. Drop by teaspoonfuls on lightly greased baking sheet. (Leave space of at least 2 inches between each cookie to allow for spreading.) Bake 10 to 15 minutes in 400°F. moderately hot oven. When cookies are cool, spread with Burnt Butter Icing. Makes 5 dozen cookies.

BURNT-BUTTER ICING

 6 *Tbs. butter*
1½ *cups confectioners sugar*
 1 *tsp. vanilla*
    hot water

Melt butter, keeping over heat until it is golden brown. Blend in confectioners sugar. Add vanilla. Stir in about 4 tablespoons of hot water until icing is the right consistency to spread smoothly.

— *Anne Lorimer*

Swedish Rosettes

To make these cookies you will need to purchase a rosette form. It is a metal stick with an iron piece that screws on and off so that you can purchase different shapes. It looks similar to a branding iron. You can purchase one of these in the gourmet gadget shop of many department stores or speciality shops.

2 eggs
2 tsp. sugar
1 cup milk
1 cup flour
½ tsp. salt
1 Tbs. lemon or orange extract
1 pint corn oil
Confectioners sugar
Rosette form

Beat eggs. Add sugar and milk. Mix together. Sift flour and salt. Add gradually to the egg mixture and beat until smooth and creamy. Add flavoring. Mix again. The batter is ready.

Use a deep fryer or 2 quart saucepan and fill half way with corn oil. Heat to 375°F. Take a tiny drop of the batter and dip it into the pot. If it sizzles, the oil is hot enough. Line the area you will be placing the cookies on well with paper towels to absorb the oil. Stick the rosette form into the oil for 15 seconds. Dry off the excess oil onto a paper towel and dip it into the batter so that you cover *only half of the form.* Once the form is coated, dip it into the hot oil. It will bubble. When the bubbling starts to slow down, check the rosette for doneness. It will turn golden brown. To remove from the form, use a fork and gently "push" the rosette around the sides until it falls off. Cool the rosettes, then sprinkle with confectioners sugar. Dip into the batter and repeat this process. Yield: about 5 dozen.

— *Catherine Arnold*

Chocolate Snowflakes

½ cup margarine or shortening
4 squares unsweetened chocolate
2 cups sugar
4 eggs
2 tsp. vanilla
2 tsp. baking powder
1½ cups flour

Melt chocolate and shortening together in a double boiler or over very low heat. Cool 5 minutes. Scrape into mixing bowl and stir in sugar. Add beaten eggs and vanilla. Add flour. Mix well. Set dough in refrigerator several hours or overnight. Then form spoonfuls into round balls, each with a diameter the size of a nickel. Roll in powdered sugar. Place 3 inches apart on greased cookie sheet. Bake 8 to 10 minutes at 375°F.

Note: Return dough to refrigerator between batches to keep cold.

Because these cookies tend to dry quickly, freezing in plastic bags is the best way to keep them. They have a delightful fudgy quality if eaten within a day after being baked or, if frozen, within a day after thawing.

— *Rosalind Hoyle Haring*

Glenda's Lemon Bars

COOKIE LAYER

1 cup flour
½ cup butter
¼ cup confectioners sugar

Mix the ingredients and press firmly into a 9 x 9-inch pan. Bake 15 minutes at 350°F.

TOPPING

2 large eggs, beaten
3 Tbs. lemon juice
1 cup sugar
½ tsp. baking powder
2 Tbs. flour

Mix well, and pour over cookie layer. Bake at 350°F. for 25 minutes, or until set. When cool, sprinkle with confectioners sugar and cut into small bars.

— *Penny V. Schwab*

Neva's Butterbrickle Bars

COOKIE LAYER

1½ cups sifted flour
¾ cup packed brown sugar
½ cup soft butter
¼ tsp. salt

Combine and mix until crumbly, then press into a 10 x 15-inch jelly roll pan. Bake at 375°F. for 10 minutes.

CANDY LAYER
(while cookie layer bakes)

1 6-oz. package butterscotch chips
2 Tbs. vegetable shortening
1 Tbs. water
pinch of salt

Combine and stir over low heat until smooth. Remove cookie layer from oven and spoon candy mixture over the top, spreading evenly. Sprinkle 1½ cups chopped nuts over the top. Return to oven and bake 10 more minutes. Cut in bars while warm. — *Penny V. Schwab*

Date-and-Apricot Bars

Note: Make date and apricot filling first, and allow to cool slightly while mixing dough for bars.

DATE-AND-APRICOT FILLING

1 cup pitted dates (cut into small pieces)
1¾ cups drained, cooked apricots unsweetened
½ cup brown or white sugar
2 Tbs. liquid drained from cooked apricots (or water)

Blend fruit with sugar and liquid in saucepan. Boil until mixture thickens (about 3 minutes). Cool slightly and use as filling for bars.

BARS

¾ cup melted shortening (half butter for flavor)
1 cup brown sugar
2 cups flour
1 tsp. soda
2 cups quick-cooking oatmeal
1 tsp. vanilla

Blend shortening with brown sugar. Sift flour before measuring. Sift flour and soda together, and mix with oatmeal. Blend this dry mixture and vanilla into brown sugar and shortening mixture, working into dough with hands. Press half of this mixture on bottom of well-greased baking pan. Spread date and apricot filling over entire surface. Top with remaining crumb mixture, pressing gently down into filling with hand or back of spoon to make crumbs stick to filling. Bake 30 minutes in 350°F. oven. Makes 32 bars.

— *Anne Lorimer*

Tea-Time Chocolate Puffs

½ cup shortening
1⅔ cup sugar
2 eggs
2 oz. baking chocolate
½ cup broken pecans
2½ cups sifted flour
2 tsp. baking powder
½ tsp. salt
⅓ cup milk
2 tsp. vanilla

Thoroughly cream together shortening and sugar. Add beaten eggs and chocolate that has been melted over low heat. Stir in pecans. Sift dry ingredients together and add alternately with milk that has been flavored with vanilla. Cover and chill for 3 hours.

Before shaping, heat oven to 350°F. Form dough into 1-inch balls, then roll in confectioners sugar.

Bake on cookie sheet in 350°F. oven for 10 minutes. Yields 60 cookies.

—*Terri Castillo*

CANDIES AND NUTS

Seven-Layer Squares

1 stick butter
1 cup graham cracker crumbs
1 3½-oz. shredded coconut
1 cup coarsely broken
    walnuts
1 6-oz. package chocolate chips
1 6-oz. package butterscotch
    chips
1 can condensed milk

Melt butter in 9 x 13-inch dish or pan. Mix in the graham cracker crumbs and spread to cover bottom of dish. Sprinkle the coconut over butter and crumb mixture. Then spread walnuts over the above. Sprinkle chocolate and butterscotch chips over all. Pour the condensed milk from corner to corner of dish, making certain that each square inch is covered. Bake in 350°F. oven for 25 minutes. Cool. Cut into squares.
— *Betty R. Schneider*

Choco-Nut Bonbons

1 cup butter or margarine,
    softened
1 15-oz. can sweetened
    condensed milk
2 1 lb. boxes powdered sugar
2 14-oz. boxes flaked coconut
1 lb. walnuts or pecans,
    finely chopped
3 6-oz. packages chocolate chips
1 block (¼ lb.) household
    paraffin

Mix together butter, condensed milk, sugar, coconut and nuts. Roll into small balls. Place on cookie sheet and chill. Melt chocolate pieces and paraffin together in saucepan on *warm*, or in double boiler. Place a toothpick in candy balls, dip in warm chocolate mixture and replace on cookie sheet for chocolate to harden. Refrigerate or freeze until needed. Yield: 250 bonbons. — *Virginia Westervelt*

"You-Got-Chocolate-On-My-Peanut Butter" Candy

12 oz. peanut butter
1 lb. confectioners sugar
1½ sticks butter (soft)
2 large-size chocolate bars

Mix together, on medium speed, peanut butter, sugar and butter, and spread in a 9 x 13-inch pan. Melt chocolate bars over low heat, stirring constantly. Smooth over pressed mixture. Refrigerate. When cooled, cut into squares.
— *Sue Monk Kid*

Peanut Butter Pinwheels

¼ lb. butter, softened
1 lb. confectioners sugar,
    sifted
½ tsp. vanilla
    milk
    peanut butter

In a large bowl, sift confectioners sugar over softened butter, reserving about ½ cup of sugar for the rolling process. Cream butter and confectioners sugar, adding milk, a few drops at a time, until the mixture sticks together to a consistency that can be rolled. Add vanilla; mix and form into a large ball. Divide fondant in two parts. Sprinkle confectioners sugar on pastry sheet or waxed paper and rolling pin. Roll each ball to ¼-inch thickness. Spread generously with peanut butter. Roll up jelly-roll fashion. Sprinkle more sugar on sheet and roll with both hands until the roll is about 1 inch in diameter. With a sharp knife, slice roll into bite-sized pieces. Store in the refrigerator.

— *Betty R. Graham*

Pecan Tassies

PASTRY

3 oz. cream cheese, softened
½ cup butter or margarine
1 cup sifted, plain flour

Blend cream cheese and butter or margarine. Stir in flour. Chill for about 1 hour. Shape into 24 one-inch balls. Place in 1¾ inch muffin tins. Press dough against sides and bottom.

FILLING

1 egg
¾ cup brown sugar
1 Tbs. soft butter or margarine
1 tsp. vanilla extract
dash of salt
⅓ cup coarsely broken pecans

Beat together egg, sugar, butter, vanilla and salt until smooth. Divide ½ of the pecans among pastry-lined cups. Spoon in egg mixture on top of pecans. Sprinkle remaining pecans on egg mixture. Bake in slow oven at 325°F. for 25 minutes or until filling is set. Cool and remove from pan. Makes 24.

— *Drue Duke*

Cream Candy

2 cups sugar
2 Tbs. vinegar
1 tsp. lemon extract
1 tsp. cream of tartar

Add a little water to moisten the sugar; boil with vinegar and cream of tartar, without stirring, until brittle when tried in cold water. Add flavoring; turn out quickly on buttered plate. When cool enough to handle, pull until white and cut into small pieces. — *Janet Shaffer*

Penuche

2 cups light brown sugar
⅓ cup milk
1 Tbs. butter
¾ cup chopped nuts
1 tsp. vanilla extract

Put sugar, milk and butter into saucepan. Boil with as little stirring as possible until it makes a soft ball in cold water. Take from fire; add nuts and vanilla; beat until thick, and pour into greased pans.

— *Janet Shaffer*

Nutty Squares

1 cup white sugar
1 cup white corn syrup
1 cup chunk-style peanut butter
6 cups toasted flakes cereal
1 6-oz. package chocolate chips
1 6-oz. package butterscotch chips

Combine sugar and syrup in top of double boiler and bring almost to a boil. Add peanut butter. Continue cooking until well mixed. Do *not* bring to boil (approx. 1 minute).

Spread 6 cups of cereal in 9 x 13-inch flat pan. Pour the cooked mixture over cereal and mix thoroughly. Pat with spatula to flatten evenly.

Melt the chocolate and butterscotch chips in top of double boiler. Frost the top of cereal mixture with this. Refrigerate. Within an hour or two, cut in 1 inch squares.

— *Betty R. Schneider*

Italian Chestnuts

1 lb. bag of chestnuts

Make 2 crosscut gashes on the flat side of each chestnut shell, using a sharp, pointed knife. Cover chestnuts with boiling water and cook for 15 minutes. Drain and remove skins. Do not overcook. Break chestnuts in half, keeping pieces as large as possible. —*Terri Castillo*

Pfeffernusse (Pepper Nuts)

Mix in a large bowl:

2 cups sugar
1 cup butter
1⅔ cups white syrup
1 tsp. cardamon
1 tsp. cloves
1 tsp. nutmeg
1 tsp. ginger
1 tsp. allspice

1 tsp. cinnamon
1 pt. sweet cream
1 egg, slightly beaten
4 tsp. baking powder
   grated orange peel, optional
   ground nuts, optional

Add enough flour to make a stiff dough. Pat 1 inch thick into flat pans and refrigerate 12 hours. Roll into balls about the size of a hickory nut and bake on a cookie sheet at 300° - 350°F. 8 to 10 minutes until golden brown. Cool and store.
— *Mickey Campbell Davis*

Sugared Walnuts

1½ cups granulated sugar
¼ cup honey
½ cup water
3 cups walnut kernels
½ tsp. vanilla extract

Combine sugar, honey and water in a saucepan and cook to 242°F., or until a little of the mixture forms a soft ball when dropped into cold water. Remove from heat. Add walnut kernels and vanilla and stir until the syrup has become creamy and thick. Turn onto waxed paper to harden, then break into individual pieces.

You may divide the syrup into 2 or 3 bowls, and color it pink, green, yellow, etc., with vegetable coloring. Before it gets too firm, drop by spoonfuls onto waxed paper.
— *Zona B. Davis*

MY OWN FAVORITE CHRISTMAS RECIPES